My *Racing* Certainties

My *Racing* Certainties

Bobby McAlpine

Quiller Press

By the same author:

One Shot at Life

Dear Eric

Hope you enjoy this

all best wishes

Bobby

ISBN 978-1-84689-223-3

First published 2015

Published by
Quiller Publishing Ltd
Wykey House
Shrewsbury
Cheshire
5Y4 1JA

Produced by JJG Publishing
Designed by Graham Hiles
Printed by Guttenberg Press, Malta

Contents

Acknowledgements

Again I must thank my editor Jeremy Greenwood and all at Quiller Publishing, my wonderful secretary Sue Davies and Roddy Bloomfield, whose advice is always invaluable.

Others who have helped me include Lord Vestey, Charles Barnett, Carolyn Elwes, Wendy Cousins, who was Robert Sangster's racing director, Peter McCalmont the honorary secretary of the Jockey Club rooms and their former manager Alan Medlock who helped my research at a critical moment. Mark Fitzgerald also contributed some advice as did many others.

I am sorry that those who have read *One Shot at Life* will find some repetition, but this book is aimed at a different readership who need some excerpts from my first book. Once again I have to emphasise that, for better or worse, every word written is my own.

The photo on the back of the jacket shows Cormorant Wood winning the Champion Stakes at Newmarket.

Chapter 1

Royalty and Racing

Anybody who invests in a racehorse is following a very illustrious group of fellow humans. Not for nothing has the sport been known as the 'Sport of Kings' and surely 'Queens' should be added to that title. A stream of monarchs have all become immersed in the sport, from Henry VIII onward. Although Henry VIII did not spend much time watching horses race each other, he did import pedigree bloodstock from Italy, mainly bought from the Duke of Mantina.

His daughter, Queen Elizabeth I, is recorded as watching horse racing at Croydon, which up until the end of the nineteenth century was quite a centre of National Hunt racing. James I attended a meeting at Lincoln and presented a trophy there and both Charles I and II had major interests in the sport. James I also attended Newmarket regularly and his love of all country sports, most of which could be indulged in the surrounds of Newmarket, led to criticism from Whitehall that the Monarch was neglecting affairs of State and spending too much time there. Although James was able to largely ignore parliament, his successor, Charles I, who did exactly the same as his father, was far less successful and could partly blame his father for the problems his stays at Newmarket brought him.

It was natural for Charles II to follow his predecessors and indulge himself at Newmarket and Charles, who never did anything by halves, found Newmarket the perfect playground. Charles's broad views of his lady loves were commented on by one biographer, who said that few monarchs could cavort with ladies as different as Louise, later Duchess of Portsmouth, who was given a magnificent suite of apartments at Newmarket, and fascinating, beguiling, Nell Gwynn, who needed less ostentatious treatment.

Both Charles I and II were good horsemen and Charles II actually rode in and won the Newmarket Town Plate twice in the 1660s. He remains the only monarch to have ridden a winner on the flat, although Edward VIII did so over the jumps. His love life made Newmarket the ideal place for him, although one mistress, Frances Stuart, eloped and married the Duke of Richmond. Charles was so angry that the Royal visit to Newmarket's spring meeting was abandoned, but he was not to be parted from his favourite playground for long. Indeed Charles II did much for the revival of horse racing in Britain, as Cromwell's protectorate had left it almost extinct, with few racehorses surviving it and Charles had to scour the continent for suitable mares to build up the Royal Stud. Charles's last visit to Newmarket was in 1684, a year before his death, and, as his biographer said, with the passing of the King passed undoubtedly some of the glory of Newmarket.

There is no record of his successor, James II, taking any interest in racing but William of Orange certainly did and attended the spring meeting at Newmarket in 1689. He was followed by Queen Anne, who did an immense amount for the sport. She had a large stud at Newmarket and raced horses, sometimes in her own name and occasionally in the name of Mr Frampton, her racing manager. She did much for both Newmarket and Ascot, was a keen and accomplished rider and loved hunting and all sporting venues involving horses. In 1702 she made the Duke of Somerset, who had encouraged her from her youth, Master of the Horse. She started the Royal Ascot meeting, though it was a later monarch, George IV, who started the Royal Procession early in the nineteenth century. In 1714 the popular Queen Anne had a winner at York but was to die the following week to be succeeded by King George I.

George I, in 1721, granted the Duke of Somerset a lease of all the Newmarket land on which the Royal Palace stood with permission to pull down any building at his own expense, but he did occasionally go to Newmarket, possibly out of a sense of duty and he did have a racing manager, Tregonwell Frampton and kept the Royal Stud going. There is little interest shown by George II though a son, the Duke of Cumberland did and bred one of the most famous horses in the history of the turf, namely Eclipse. Not George III but his son, the Prince of Wales and later George IV, was an enthusiastic supporter of racing and stayed in Newmarket frequently until 1791, when he had a row with the Jockey Club over the running of one of his horses. However, when he succeeded to the throne he had the Royal Palace at Newmarket repaired, although it was never anywhere near the former glorious building of the Stuarts. In fact it was put up for sale by Queen Victoria in the 1850s and pulled down shortly afterwards.

From 1784 to 1792 George IV won 185 races but on October 21st 1791 his horse, Escape, ran in a field of four at Newmarket with Sam Chifney on board. Escape had not worked for a fortnight and was not fit and neither the prince nor jockey backed him and he duly finished last of four. The decision was made to run him the next day over a completely different distance – two miles the first day and nearly four the second. Escape won easily at 5/1 in the betting, with two of the horses he had been beaten by the day before behind him. Both Prince and jockey had taken advantage of the generous price and backed him. The Stewards of the Jockey Club held a lengthy enquiry which included looking at Chifney's betting book. In those days jockeys were allowed to bet and their wagers were recorded. Later they told His Royal Highness that if Chifney rode his horses again 'no gentleman would start against him'. A polite way of warning Chifney off.

The Stewards were Sir Charles Bunbury, Mr Dutton and Mr Thomas Panton, a remarkably unaristocratic trio for the time and a trio determined to act for the good of racing. Nevertheless, the result was to send the Prince of Wales into a furious sulk from which he never totally emerged. He awarded Chifney, who had a poor reputation, a pension of £200 and he sold his stud. Although there was no evidence that anybody benefited financially from the incident – Chifney only had 20 guineas on the second race and Escape was known to have two ways of running – it was historically a great triumph for the Jockey Club, who had stood up to Royalty under the most difficult circumstances. It was not until 1805 that they attempted to placate the Prince of Wales, when they sent him a message that they deeply regretted his absence from Newmarket and sincerely hoped he might return. The message got a polite reply but the Prince, still furious at the treatment he had received, probably had no intentions of doing so. Years later, when a suggestion was made that a horse of his should take part in a match at Newmarket, he said to William Chifney, who trained for him, 'No William, they treated your father and me very badly, I won't run there.'

Whilst Newmarket was to suffer from the Royal wrath, the other important racecourses of the period continued to receive its patronage – Ascot, Epsom, York, Doncaster and Chester.

In 1825, George IV instituted the Royal Procession at Ascot, an event of enormous importance to racing which was to make a great contribution of great benefit to Ascot in the years to come. It was not the next monarch, Queen Victoria, who was to stamp herself in racing history but her son Edward, Prince of Wales, who took to the turf like a duck to water and indeed there are many similarities between the racing careers of George IV and Edward VII.

In both cases as Prince of Wales they had very poor relationships with their parents and in Edward VII's case, his mother's refusal to let him participate in any affairs of state pushed him further into the arms of an array of friends who loved the turf and soon had him feeling the same way. Although his own relationship with his children was far from perfect he did encourage them to enjoy racing and both King George V and VI were to become enthusiastic owners.

The Jockey Club was determined not to have a repeat of the appalling row that caused such problems with George IV and they persuaded the Prince of Wales to become a member as early as possible. He attended meetings and although the proceedings were not written down verbatim his influence must have been considerable. He was the only monarch who was an active member of the Jockey Club.

His first winner was Leonidas, at the now defunct course at Aldershot, and it was watched by his mother. His colours were not registered until 1875 and in deference to his mother's views he started racing by buying cheap horses and running them at small meetings. He started the Sandringham Stud in 1885 and had a few horses with John Porter at Kingsclere and in 1893 he went to Dick Marsh at Newmarket. When Persimmon, ridden by Jack Watts and trained by Marsh, won the Derby in 1896, he received a fantastic reception, one commentator going as far as saying it was the high point of the popularity of the English Royal Family. It is interesting that Persimmon, who went on to win the St Leger, had a very difficult preparation and his owner was persuaded, early in the season, to miss the 2,000 Guineas and concentrate on the Derby. His early work gave no encouragement but Dick Marsh always thought the horse had great potential and his final gallop was more encouraging and was watched by, amongst others, the future King George V and his wife. Persimmon turned out to be as fine a sire as he was racehorse. Kept in training as a four-year-old, he won the Ascot Gold Cup over two-and-a-half miles and then the Eclipse over half that distance. As a sire his greatest offspring was a daughter called Sceptre, who won four classics and would have had an even greater career had she not been owned by Bob Sievier, an insatiable gambler who put his wagering before his horses' interests. The Prince of Wales was fortunate that his mare Perdita II bred a third colt by Persimmon, which he named Diamond Jubilee, after the 60th anniversary of his mother's reign. He had marvellous conformation but, though pampered from birth, he grew up not to have a good temperament like his sire and he hated any jockey that was put up on him. Jack Watts soon gave up but Morny Cannon, his successor, managed him for a bit until the horse, in the spring of 1900, turned on Cannon and, just before the 2000 Guineas after riding work and when he tried to lead the colt home, he was rolled to the ground and would have been killed if others had not come to the rescue in the nick of time. Not surprisingly Cannon refused to ride him again, so Dick Marsh was faced with a situation which he solved by putting up an inexperienced young lad, Bertie Jones, who rode him in regular work. Jones succeeded in winning not only the 2000 Guineas but the Derby and the St Leger – the prized triple crown – for his Royal master.

When Edward VII came to the throne he went through one of those lean periods well known to our current monarch and it was not until the end of his reign when Minoru won the Derby of 1909. He is still the only horse to have won the race for a reigning monarch and he won it, with Bertie Jones up, by the shortest of short heads. The crowd gave the King a fantastic reception; he was immensely popular.

His eldest son, King George V, will probably be best remembered for the Derby of 1913, when a leading suffragette of the day, Emily Davison, ran across the course into the King's horse, Anmer, and was killed. Although commentators today all claim it was a deliberate act, neither Herbert Jones, who rode Anmer, nor Steve Donoghue, the leading jockey of the day, who gave evidence, believe the act was deliberate. Herbert Jones believed that as Anmer was well behind, Davison thought the race was over and she could cross the course. Donoghue maintained that to single out a horse would have been impossible. The race was also notable for one of the most controversial Stewards' decisions ever, when the winner, Craganour, the favourite, was disqualified and a hundred-to-one outsider, Aboyeur, given the race.

Racing was severely curtailed by the Great War of 1914-18 but as the twenties progressed King George's eldest son, Edward, Prince of Wales, became an enthusiastic horseman, both in the hunting field and over jumps in National Hunt racing. He won a race at Hawthorn Hill in 1921 and again in 1923 on Pet Dog. Riding in the same race in 1928 he fell at the first fence and, although only slightly injured, questions were asked in Parliament and following a meeting with the Prime Minister, he gave up both hunting and race riding and lost all interest in the sport.

The Second World War coincided with the racing careers of King George VI's best two horses, Sun Chariot and Big Game, both leased from the National Stud. They were both unbeaten as two-year-olds and finished their two-year-old season jointly at the top of the Free Handicap.

In 1942 their three-year-old careers started well, with Big Game winning the 2000 Guineas and Sun Chariot the 1000 Guineas. The Derby and Oaks were run at Newmarket not Epsom and the Oaks, run first, was duly won by Sun Chariot but Big Game was beaten, at odds on, in the Derby and his jockey, Gordon Richards, was convinced he did not stay the mile-and-a-half. He won the Champion Stakes and retired to stud, his only defeat being in the Derby. Sun Chariot won the St Leger, easily beating the first and second in the Derby and Gordon Richards was convinced she would have won most Derbys, although whether she would have acted as well at Epsom as she did at Newmarket we will never know.

For those of us whose fascination with racing dates from the late forties, it is the wife of King George VI, the Queen Mother, and her daughter, our reigning monarch, whose extensive racing interests have done so much to excite the public.

Sadly the Queen Mother will be best remembered, not for her many winners in the National Hunt field, but for her disastrous loss in the Grand National, when Devon Loch came to grief a hundred yards from the finishing line, having looked certain to win the race by a wide margin. Dick Francis, his jockey, became a good friend of mine and used to lunch with us every year on the Friday before the National. I often discussed what had happened that day and he always said that the horse's collapse was a complete mystery. He did say that the wall of noise from the crowd which greeted him as he reached the final straight was something he had never encountered before and perhaps the horse stopped momentarily and seized up, but he was far from sure that was the real reason.

The Queen Mother's reputedly favourite course was Sandown but she also loved Cheltenham and the race there at the festival named after her, the Queen Mother Champion Chase, which is their most important race after the Gold Cup. My sister, Valerie, was part owner with Willy Jenks and John Edwards was the trainer of Pearlyman; they won the race twice.

The Queen Mother had many good chasers but it was not just the racehorses that did so much to excite the public. The sight of Her Majesty at a racecourse really cheered people up. She was obviously enjoying herself, loved a drink and got a lot of pleasure out of every meeting she attended. I remember her particularly at Royal Ascot, where she would ride in her buggy, driven by her loyal attendant and smile at the admiring throng, all making way for her. The fact that she was in such good health and got to her hundredth birthday still active, must encourage many lesser mortals like myself to think there is a slim chance we can do the same.

Although her great horses were chasers, she left a significant legacy after her death, when her horses in training and her mares went into the ownership of the Queen, who went from becoming an owner purely on the flat to one under both rules. Very good news for racing.

The Queen had shown a passion for racing at an early age; no doubt her parent's good horses, like Big Game and Sun Chariot, helped but children often do not follow the interests of their parents and British horseracing is very fortunate in this respect. It is always a help to get a really good horse early on and I know that Her Majesty considers Aureole the best horse she ever owned, though she did not breed him. Aureole had won the Lingfield Derby Trial and was strongly fancied for the Derby. He was extremely unlucky to run into Pinza, who according to Gordon Richards was one of the two best horses he ever rode – Sun Chariot being the other. Aureole finished a gallant second but Gordon Richards never had any real worries and Her Majesty was to congratulate in the winners' enclosure a jockey she had just knighted.

Her other good horses include: Above Suspicion, Almeria, Dunfermline, Height of Fashion, Highclere, Unknown Quantity and now Estimate. She has won all the classics except the Derby and was leading owner on the flat as early as 1954. Her racing managers were first Sir Charles Moore, for a long time Lord Porchester and now John Warren, who is Lord Carnarvon's son-in-law.

I never met the Queen Mother but I have met the Queen on several occasions, the first when she presented me with the Ascot Gold Cup in 1970. Strangely the most animated conversation I had was when she, with Prince Philip, opened a new civic centre in Manchester, the UNEX Building, where my old company was the contractor. Her Majesty arrived in front of me after a number of civic dignitaries had been presented and Robert Fellowes, her principal secretary, said, 'Your Majesty, Bobby McAlpine, who has sadly lost one of your favourite horses, Sagaro (a triple Ascot Gold Cup winner), who was standing at his stud.' Sagaro actually died covering his third mare! To my amazement the Queen became very animated and after the commiserations over Sagaro a general discussion followed for several minutes, which must have amazed the dignitaries behind her from the Home Secretary downwards. Her relief at finding someone who could converse on her favourite sport was obvious. So is her enjoyment at her own meeting, Royal Ascot, which I was lucky to witness at fairly close quarters when the Jockey Club stand used to overlook the Royal Box before the rebuild.

Nobody cheered louder than me when Estimate won the Queen's Vase and the following year the Ascot Gold Cup. Her Majesty loves long distance races and having myself won the two longest at the Royal Meeting, the Ascot Gold Cup and the Queen Alexandra, I find it splendid that the Monarch does not follow the current fashion that speed is all important.

She follows a long line of Kings and Queens who have helped to make our sport what it is today and I am sure she will continue to do so for some years to come. Royalty and racing have been together for several centuries; long may it last.

Chapter 2

Early Days

My first appearance on a racecourse was at Chester for the first day of the May meeting the year after the war ended. I should have been at Harrow for the start of the summer term but had contracted chicken pox during the holidays and I persuaded mother to delay my departure for a couple of days so that I could go to the races. I remember a vast crowd, which is not surprising as there were over 100,000 people on Cup day, and my mother introducing me to a jockey who she thought was Tommy Weston but was in fact Michael Beary. The outing set back my cricket career at Harrow as I missed the early nets and went into a trial for the junior colts totally unprepared and performed poorly.

A year later, Arthur Straker, the father of Ivan Straker, who was the English boss of Seagrams and did an enormous amount for Aintree when I became a director, including being the Grand National Sponsor, took my mother and I to Haydock. I can't honestly say that at this point my pulses had been set on fire but shortly after leaving school a small group of us started going to local meetings and I was soon addicted to the dangerous game of backing horses. I was also aware that some of my family were important owners – for instance Sir Malcolm McAlpine, who I called Uncle Tom, had won the Grand National in 1921 with Shaun Spadah, who was the only finisher, although two others were remounted to fill the places. The RSPCA would have had a field day!

When my mother moved to London with her second husband, my brother Billy and I caught a Greenline bus and made our way to Uncle Tom's house at Fairmile, near Cobham. There he would show us photographs of the great race and fire up my enthusiasm.

My grandfather was also a keen owner, though not a successful one, but I had for a number of years his trophies, large silver cups won at courses from Perth to Oswestry and Llanamynech, also numerous photographs. Sadly the trophies were stolen in a burglary comparatively recently though my main trophies, the Ascot Gold Cup, Champion Stakes and Benson and Hedges china were all locked in the safe.

Father never had the slightest desire to become an owner; he frequently told a story about when my grandfather went on a long holiday to Madeira to recuperate from a serious illness. He was immediately rung up by my grandfather's trainer, Max Barthrop, who said that he was owed three months training bills, which father duly paid. When my grandfather returned father met him at the quayside and after a short interval father brought up the training fees. 'You idiot Jimmy,' said my grandfather, 'I paid him six months in advance; let that be a lesson to you.'

Although father would never become an owner he liked the party atmosphere around local racing and became a shareholder at Chester and a member of Bangor-on-Dee, his two local meetings.

I might well have followed father and become a moderately keen racegoer at local meetings had it not been for a cricket match at which Ian Lomax, who held a licence for his wife Rosemary, was playing. The party afterwards went on to the early hours and I woke up with one of my worst hangovers and the terrible memory that, in those alcohol fuelled early hours, I had agreed to buy a racehorse. The words 'racing is a rich man's sport' echoed in my ears, as I had no other money than my fairly modest salary. I dashed to the phone and managed to get hold of Rosemary, who told me the horse had left Ireland two hours ago and I could come and see him when I liked. My next move was to ring my brother, Billy, to tell him that he had acquired half a racehorse and to his credit he agreed to come in. The one thing in our favour was the horse, a four-year-old gelding called Marnrack, was ready to run and a fortnight later Billy and I drove down to Chepstow to see him run in my colours which closely resembled my grandfather's and incorporated the family tartan. Neither Ian nor Rosemary were at Chepstow but we had a number of friends there and, to my surprise, Marnrack nearly won the race, a maiden hurdle, being beaten half a length after challenging the winner through the last two furlongs. The excitement of seeing your first runner in your own colours run so well was incredible and from that moment on I was hooked on racehorse ownership. I often wonder what would have happened if the horse had been hopeless. Neither Billy nor I could have afforded to race him for long and, although I would have missed out on a lot of fun, I might have got to my advancing years a much richer man! Interestingly Kevin Prendegast who sold Marnrack to us is still training today.

As Billy and I could only race on Saturdays, we made Rosemary wait for a couple of weeks and then set sail for Uttoxeter, where Marnrack was a hot favourite for the first race. Unfortunately when we got to the venue the town was enveloped in fog. We made for the bar at the White

Hart, a favourite watering hole, where the sad news came through that the meeting had been abandoned. The fog quickly cleared and at the time of the first race conditions would have been perfect. Rosemary then wanted to run him at Wincanton mid-week and as neither Billy or I dared take a mid-week day off we were not able to see our first win. In fact it transpired that he won despite a terrible mistake and Peter Pickford, our jockey, did extremely well to stay aboard. His jumping was always a problem. For instance two years later he was in a £10,000 race at Manchester and cruising in front, when he hit the second last causing his apprentice, a last-minute substitute for Pickford, to fall. Ten thousand pounds is still a lot of money but it was probably worth nearer a hundred thousand in those days.

As Marnrack was paying his way I decided to have another horse and Rosemary and I set off for the yearling sales at Deauville; the only time I have ever visited that particular sale. A number of us from Shropshire had visited Le Touquet and the glamorous casino there. We stayed at a motel and every morning went to a large bar called Flavio's, where I witnessed an amazing bet between two of our party: who could drink a bottle of champagne put into a pint tankard and eat two peeled, boiled eggs quickest. The bet was a hundred pounds and was fascinating to watch as the first egg disappeared quickly but the second caused problems and the champagne won by a short head only for the drinker to vomit most of it over the bar floor! The bar owner took it all in good humour and the celebration continued.

The Deauville casino was larger but slightly less glamorous but I did witness three of Britain's leading trainers playing Baccarat for extremely high stakes. At the sale our pockets did not reach ninety percent of the yearlings, but we did end up with a small, neat filly called La Foire II. When we got her back to England Ian Lomax accused us of getting totally pissed and coming back with a pony. In fact La Foire II was to win nine races and started favourite for the Cesarewitch, in which she was hampered. Sadly she got a bad cut when she went to stud, which became infected and eventually she had to be put down. A sad end for the first mare I tried to breed from.

My propulsion from owning horses in the minor leagues to the big races came when Rosemary bought me a grey or roan colt at the yearling sales. I had asked her to buy a horse who could be a speedy two-year-old and her purchase of a yearling by an unfashionable sire out of Grecian Garden, didn't seem to fit the bill at all. I called him Precipice Wood after the best stand at our shoot at Llanarmon. In fact he did show considerable ability as a two-year-old coming third to Hotfoot in the Fenwolf Stakes. He was ridden in all three two-year-old races by Bill Rickaby, who was a great hero of mine, having ridden Uncle Tom's classic winner, Zabara, in the 1,000 Guineas. Sadly he was in his last season and Precipice Wood's third run was the last he was to ride for me. The race was a very disappointing one and Precipice Wood's nose was streaming after the race. He was obviously not right and in the present day vets would have immediately spotted that he had a virus and he would have been scoped and not allowed to race. Things have certainly moved a long way in the veterinary world and we were very fortunate that irretrievable damage was not done by the run. Some years later another good horse, River Ceiriog, ran a similar race with a runny nose and I believed he was never quite as good after it.

Rosemary took on a new jockey, David Yates, a former champion apprentice, whose nickname was 'flapper'. As Precipice Wood had been entered for the Derby we ran him in a trial at Goodwood, where he came second to a filly who was relatively unknown. We withdrew him from the Derby and ran him in a small race at Thirsk, which he won by so far that I wondered if we had made the right decision and when the filly, who had beaten him at Goodwood, came second in the Oaks, my doubts increased. The next race was the King George V handicap at Royal Ascot, where Paul Cook took over as Jockey, for reasons I don't remember, and won by ten lengths, easing up throughout the last two furlongs.

We were confident about winning his next race, the Geoffrey Freer Stakes, a group two stakes at Newbury. I could not go because I was the manager and captain of the Harrow Wanderers cricket team against the Eton Ramblers on Evelyn Rothchild's lovely ground in Buckinghamshire. I had taken a portable television set with me to watch the race just before I was due to bat. Precipice Wood looked sure to win but was run out of it in the last fifty yards, my doubts about David Yates increased and to make matters worse my innings did not last long.

If I had concerns before the St Leger, the race Yates rode at Doncaster, finished the association for good. He got into trouble trying to come through and had a barging match with Blakeney all the way up the straight, finishing fourth with Blakeney just behind. A stewards enquiry followed and they felt, correctly in my opinion, that Yates and Ernie Johnson, on Blakeney, had equally contributed and they left the result unaltered.

The following year I insisted on having Jimmy Lindley as my jockey, although Rosemary, who felt sorry for Yates, started prevaricating. She was a wonderful trainer but man management was not her strong point – if only Ian her husband had been more supportive she might have gone right to the top.

The first race selected was the John Porter at Newbury, where Torpid, who got first run in a slowly run race, turned out a surprise winner, but the Paradise Stakes at Newmarket, run on very firm ground, was a different story and Precipice beat a great stayer, High Line, reasonably decisively.

The race was probably not run to suit either of them, turning into a four furlong sprint after an initial crawl, and Joe Mercer, High Line's jockey, challenged me to a large bet for the next time they met. The bet was accepted but the meeting never took place as the leg problems that finished Precipice Wood's career started manifesting themselves.

It is worth saying at this point that watering systems were in their infancy and in a hot summer horses often had to run on unsuitably firm ground. Rosemary was now faced with the problem of getting her star horse to the Gold Cup at Ascot sufficiently fit to stand a chance of winning.

Lambourn was also far from being the training centre it is now and the communal gallops there were certainly not ideal. Uncle Robin kindly offered the use of his gallop at Newmarket but it was Derrick Candy, the father of Henry, who let us use his, easily the best in Lambourn at the time.

The weeks before the Gold Cup were a worrying time and Rosemary and I rang each other up every other day. However the great day arrived and all seemed well. Precipice looked very well and was perfectly calm until Jimmy Lindley got on board, when he suddenly reared up (having been stung by a bee) unseated Jimmy and bolted towards the High Street. Frankly I thought all was lost and I was terrified the horse would be badly injured. However he was retrieved and seemed none the worse and Jimmy was reunited with him and they set off for a delayed start. I could hardly watch the proceedings but I will never forget the commentator, Michael Seth-Smith, who had become a good friend, raising his voice as they entered the final straight: Precipice Wood has started his run and has gone into the lead; in fact he and Blakeney had a desperate tussle all the way to the line but we prevailed by half a length. The race was on bone hard ground which nearly finished off Precipice's tendons but the win was very popular with the crowd and a tremendous celebration ensued. I was informed that Her Majesty would present the cup in the Royal Box and, surrounded by friends in the Irish Bar, where we had a large table, the head waiter and Jane tried to clean me up for the presentation; not an easy task as I was drenched in sweat. In fact Her Majesty was obviously tired; she had, the day before, to greet an incoming Prime Minister, Edward Heath. The race had been run on a Saturday because the general election had been on the Thursday and she had hosted a late party at Windsor the night before. Although Anne, Duchess of Westminster, who I knew well, was by her side, the conversation was a little stilted and Rosemary, the first lady trainer to win a major group one race, did not receive the congratulations the Monarch would normally have bestowed. I have been presented to Her Majesty a few times since and each time she was charming, animated and on one occasion positively overflowing with conversation.

We returned to the Irish Bar where friends were arriving from all corners of the course. The Irish Bar was a great meeting place, where members could meet friends. It became the main dining room for the Ascot Racing Club and was destroyed when the new stand was built. I always thought its loss was a great mistake as I loved the atmosphere there.

Precipice now had the choice of two races, the Goodwood Cup or the Prix Kergorlay at Deauville. Rosemary left the decision to me and whilst Jimmy was very anti Deauville, I was very pro on the grounds that the race was over a distance half a mile shorter which would help when the horse went to stud. Jimmy argued that the track would not suit and the French jockeys would block us. In the event he was right except that it was the genius of an English jockey, Lester Piggott, no less, that undid us. It was another blazing hot day and the course was half in sun, half in shadow. Lester Piggott on Reindeer, trained by Vincent O'Brien, lost a couple of places on the final bend to come in shadow on the stand side, unseen by Jimmy and Precipice who thought the race was won. We should have won and sadly it was to be his last race, the suspect tendon giving way a few days afterwards.

Despite the sadness of Deauville I had a wonderful year. At the age of thirty-nine I had won the Ascot Gold Cup with a top-class horse. I could also look back on a number of other horses which had given me a great deal of pleasure.

Following Precipice Wood's enforced retirement, I set about trying to make a success of him as a stallion and on Doug Francis's advice I stood him at Emral near Bangor where the owners, a married couple, Pat and Jean Broad, were close friends of Doug. I also took a share in the land involved. There was really no problem in filling the forty shares that were put on offer. I kept six for myself and several friends immediately came in and Uncle Robin and Philip Leverhulme bought a share each. Initially he was quite successful on the flat having five two-year-old winners and a good flat horse which I sent to South Africa,

Precipitack, who finished second in all three of South Africa's main staying races. I had a trainer in Johannesburg, who I subsequently fell out with, who put up an apprentice in one of the three races, which was the closest he was to lose by – a short head. The rider and trainer were strongly criticised by the main racing correspondent in Johannesburg but it was very difficult for me, still lacking in knowledge and unable to influence decisions from England.

Had I known more about breeding I would have realised that his success was always going to be as a National Hunt stallion and his best ever animal was one of the worst disasters I have had. I bought several mares to send to him and one bred a filly I called Precipienne, who was trained by the Rimells who did not think she was genuine. At that time Preciptack was also having a poor season in South Africa with a different trainer so I decided I had to cut down. Having arranged the mating of Precipienne's dam to Precipice Wood I sold her for a very small sum. When Preciptack did so much better I realised the sale was foolish and had the opportunity of buying the yearling back when he came up at Doncaster Sales, run by my good friend Harry Beeby. I had a business appointment I didn't want to miss and Doug Francis offered to go in my place. Just get him back, I said, and don't worry about the price. Doug never gave me a satisfactory answer as to why he didn't buy him for £4,000 less than I was expecting to pay; he must have been badly distracted. I immediately rang Harry Beeby and offered to give the Irish buyer a hefty profit but the horse had gone to Ireland and the buyer wanted to keep him. Two years later he failed to win his first two bumpers but the buyer had a major gamble on the third, which he won easily. He then rang me up and offered me the well named Forgive and Forget, for twenty-five thousand Irish Punts. I was stupid enough to tell in graphic detail what he could do with that sum and then had to sit by as he was sold for nearly forty thousand and was to win the 1983 Coral Golden Hurdle Final and the 1985 Cheltenham Gold Cup. He would almost certainly have won a second had he not slipped up three fences from home when in a comfortable lead and was sadly put down afterwards. A most unhappy story for me; I did not even go down as the breeder, having sold Forgive and Forget 'in utero'.

Precipice himself did really well but I stupidly sent him to Ireland for a year, where he contracted the bug which was to eventually kill him. Six years after his death I picked up the second of two large silver cups that the Thoroughbred Breeders Association gave for the champion National Hunt stallion of the year.

I cannot let the sixties go without mentioning another trainer, Pat Rohan, who had married Mary Dutton, the niece of Jack Bissell, a great friend of my father, who had been very kind to me. He had horses with Billy Dutton and urged me to do the same. Billy Dutton died suddenly and Pat, married to his daughter, went from being assistant trainer to trainer of a substantial number of horses at Malton, an East Yorkshire town. Pat had a lot of ability and had a lot of knowledge but to say he was highly strung would have been an understatement. He was a dedicated teetotaller and I often wondered what would have happened if he had had a drink. Would it have quietened him or sent him straight to the Priory? We had two or three good, fast horses, named, like Precipice, after Llanarmon woods and the two I remember best being Stunog Wood and Oswestry Covert. Pat was very adamant about jockeys and Johnny Seagrave, the stable jockey, was competent enough, if a little towards the veteran stage. He managed to get Stunog Wood left at the start at Aintree, still a mixed meeting, at five to two on and Robert Sangster and I went up to Ayr to recoup our bets. I had lost my nerve but Robert had a hefty bet and then two more as the price went out, Robert telling me how strong the market was. What neither of us knew but the bookies did, was that Seagrave had flu – but he managed to steer the filly home before taking to his bed. She went on to win the Lily Agnes at the Chester festival and she should, in my opinion, have come second to Waterloo (who won by ten lengths) in the Queen Mary at Royal Ascot, where Seagrave got her boxed in and finished fourth instead of second. One of the last horses I had with Pat was Quarry Wood, the dam of Cormorant Wood, who won a long distance, three-year-old novice race at Redcar and would have been fourth in the Chester Cup if the apprentice Pat insisted on putting up had not dropped his hands well before the post, not realising that prizes for fourth had just come in that season.

It was still early days!

Chapter 3

My Love Affair with Cartmel

I cannot remember the exact year I first went to Cartmel but it would have been in the early sixties, to run one of my first jumpers, probably Codine. The town of Cartmel is one of the most attractive in the country with a famous old Abbey and a number of ancient buildings to attract tourists. It is set in beautiful countryside at the southern end of the Lake District and just outside the town is the racecourse.

Unfortunately, in the era before motorway construction transformed that part of the country, the journey on a bank holiday was appalling and it took us three hours plus to get there. The approach around the town was particularly difficult, down narrow roads with long queues before arrival at the track.

The racecourse is not particularly exciting on arrival, mainly because you can't see most of it. A fairground emitting a lot of noise is on the far side and there is a lot of activity as you finally reach the car parks. I have to say, first impressions were not great and little did I know when I got out of my car after the appalling journey from Cheshire, that this was a course I would fall in love with.

It is difficult to imagine in this age of racecourse excellence just how primitive things were at a backward, rustic course like Cartmel in the sixties. My first appearance was to watch my horse run and to be honest I do not remember the race result but I do remember an invitation being issued to go to Col Pain's tent to have a glass of champagne. Colonel Pain was in charge of the racecourse, which I imagined belonged to him rather than the Cavendish family, the real owners.

Colonel Pain's tent had excellent champagne and I stayed there well after racing finished to stock up for the dreaded journey home. Again many readers may not realise that in the pre breathalyser era, driving with large amounts of alcohol inside you was commonplace and little thought was given by most of us as to whether our driving ability would be impaired. Anyway I left the tent with a plea from the Colonel to come again next year and please come to the tent at the beginning of racing not later on.

The following year I arrived before racing started and made for the small wooden stand, where you could get a marginally better view of part of the course. I found George Owen, a well-known National Hunt trainer, who lived near me in Cheshire and was a great friend of Doug Francis. As neither of us could see anything that happened on the last bend and as there was no steward there either we were not particularly surprised to hear the bell rung for an objection after the first race, which was overruled. The same thing happened after the second and I said jocularly to George, 'The Stewards will be getting thirsty with all this work.' The third race was George's turn to have a runner, a top hunter-chaser, Happy Morn II, usually ridden by an old school friend of mine, John Barlow. On this occasion, as John was not able to make it, Tony Biddlecombe, amateur brother of champion National Hunt jockey, Terry, took the mount. I knew George fancied the horse a lot and I had backed him accordingly. He came into view fifteen lengths in front and won pulling up. 'At least George,' I said, 'there can't be an enquiry this time,' as I strode off to the Pain tent to celebrate. I had almost reached my destination when the bell went, 'Stewards' enquiry'. Incredulously, I waited outside the tent and a few minutes later the announcement came, objection sustained, the placing's now are etc., etc. I rushed back to find a very shaken George, 'You won't believe this Bobby but Tony has a terrible stutter. Asked if he had crossed the second he said yes I did sir. He was about to say but I was ten lengths ahead but they never gave him time to get the words out.'

I was the right end of an even more bizarre decision, when Marieson ran in a hurdle race and although Anthony Johnson, my co-owner, who had taken up race riding, was there, he had agreed Roy Edwards should ride him. Coming into the straight he looked sure to win but he appeared to be caught just before the finishing line and to be beaten by about a neck. I went discontentedly to the refreshment tent when an announcement was made, 'The judge has reversed his decision and the result now is Marieson first etc.' I tore back to the winner's enclosure to find a grinning Roy Edwards, 'As I crossed the finishing line I shouted to Eric Cousins's apprentice on the other horse, I have beaten you. The judge comes up to us both and I said you got that wrong, I definitely won. He turns to the apprentice. If Mr Edwards said he won sir, I'm sure he did.' The champagne tasted even better after that.

Stories about the stewarding at Cartmel had begun to reach the ears of the Jockey Club officials at Portman Square and eventually the senior stipendiary, Mr Christian, was sent to the meeting. As it happened, Decode, Codine's first foal, was our runner and Jimmy Bourke, who had become Doug Francis's first choice of jump jockey, was down to ride her. Decode was better than her mother but a much more difficult ride and went so far wide at the far bend that she went through a patch of bluebells before rejoining the others, some lengths behind. Last into the last turn she appeared to have no chance but emerged into view in fourth place, made up a lot of ground and just got up to win. An enquiry was held not, as I expected, into the running of the race (I wasn't sure if she had stayed on the course) but into the improvement in form since her last hurdles start.

Doug and I were sat in a little anteroom, where we could hear every word Mr Christian said to the Senior Steward, as he told him the questions he should ask. Doug, who was enjoying himself enormously, waited until nearly the end of the enquiry and said to Mr Christian, 'Have you got a flat form book? Because if you have, look up the results at Haydock on Monday and you will find she came a close third on the flat there.' Collapse of enquiry!

Other Cartmel enquiries were of more public interest. The main one being the Gay Future case, where this good horse was switched for a rank outsider and small amounts of money were put on all over the country. The bookies smelt a rat but the trainer, Tony Collins, escaped jail but was merely 'warned off' all racecourses for five years. Cartmel was chosen by Collins as it had no 'blower' system in those days and it certainly hit the international racing headlines.

Before my old company built the Preston to Lancashire motorway the journey took so long we all decided to stay the night before, closer to the course, and selected a large five-star hotel just outside Blackpool. We had an excellent dinner and I ordered two bottles of vintage port. 'We don't get much demand these days,' said the waiter, 'I'll go to the cellar and see what we have.' He returned with two cobweb-covered bottles and said, 'These have been here forever, have them on the house.' They turned out, when the corks were drawn, to be Taylors 1927, arguably the finest port of the century!

The Preston to Lancashire section of the M6 motorway was started in 1963 and finished in the summer of 1965. In 1965 we set off in two Bentleys, myself and Johnny Phillipson, the owner driver of the second, driving along twenty miles of compacted stone, known as 'crusher run' prior to the tarmac being laid. The two cars sped at a hundred miles an hour with clouds of white dust floating behind. As I could not make Monday, Jane made the same journey, accompanied by Doug Francis. A member of the works management team stopped them and asked what they were doing. 'I'm Mrs McAlpine,' said Jane and I'm Jesus Christ, was the answer!

Not all the drinking was done on the course. On one occasion we were asked to have a drink after racing with a young couple who gave us their address. We all ended up at one of the largest country houses I have ever seen; I forgot to ask the name. Another time we all decided to have a drink at a nice looking pub we had passed on the outskirts of Cartmel. Peter Thompson and I had ten people crammed in two large cars. We found a convivial group who turned out to be nine off-duty Lancashire police. When last orders came, one of them said we will escort you off our patch. Five motorcyclists went in front and four behind. When they got to the border they peeled off, saluting us as they went, the last one shouting, 'Be careful, you are on your own now.'

The winners continued to flow but I sadly was not there. I was running a cricket match when I had my one and only treble, Decode, Marieson and Ginger Nut, on Monday and Jane and Doug had to celebrate without me.

When I started having horses with John Edwards, he enjoyed going to Cartmel as much as I did. Our first runner was a disaster as John had insisted on giving the ride to his attractive young assistant, Venetia Williams. She jumped the first ok, hit the second and became unbalanced and came off forty yards after the hurdle. The horse was five to two on and I was far from pleased as poor Venetia was carted off to hospital.

The following year I had another fancied horse and John announced he had engaged a young Irish amateur to ride him. 'You had better have a large bet to cover the chartered flight.' My fury was such that the teenage Irish amateur received a poor welcome. He rode a perfect race and won fairly easily. His name was Norman Williamson and it was to be the first of hundreds of rides in England for the future champion. He always rode for me wherever possible.

John, like myself, regarded Cartmel as a great party and one year I arrived to find him in great pain, perspiring freely, gripped with gout. He and his wife Gina had separated and he had arranged to meet three separate ladies at various points on the course. 'Can you find them for me and give them the bad news?' he asked. Very leg weary I found the first two but the third was never located.

The journey had got better as I was eventually able to hire the company plane and land about eight miles from the course, on a private runway. The runway was fine but sheep were allowed to roam over it and on one occasion we had to fly low over the sheep to move them off it. The taxi we hired had a driver who knew all the short cuts and I only wish we had met at the beginning not towards the end of my trips to Cartmel.

We had all had a wonderful time there through the sixties and seventies but by the eighties I was going less. Colonel Pain's great reign was over and he had handed over to his son, a charming man but the champagne stopped making its appearance until the last race. I felt I should leave a memento and bought a large cup to be presented after a chase I had won there, known as the McAlpine Cup.

Hugh Cavendish kindly asked me back to lunch at the beginning of the current century. I thought I had allowed plenty of time but the M6, which had made the journey so much shorter, had a twelve mile tailback. I was three-quarters of an hour late, much to the displeasure of my host, nor did anyone rush to get me a drink. They did offer to let me present the cup, which was in its last year of existence, but I felt the sponsor should do it. I visited the wonderful fish tent where we always had lunch, fresh from Morecombe Bay, lobsters, crabs, oysters and salmon – amazingly none of the directors knew of its existence.

I hope I shall have a reason to go to Cartmel again; it is a unique course and anybody who really loves National Hunt racing should pay it a visit. I will never forget the fun we all had there. Racing should be all about having fun, goodness knows it is expensive enough these days.

Chapter 4

The Pattern

Although the Pattern covers all the main races in Europe, it gets relatively little media coverage and most racegoers have little idea how it is financed and what rules govern its structure.

The Pattern – Group one, two, three and Listed races – was a British initiative to make a framework or 'pattern' establishing a standard at the top end of racing. This was needed for the growing internationalism of horseracing as air travel enabled horses to get speedily around Europe. The committee which started it was headed by the Duke of Norfolk with Geoffrey Freer and Peter Willett; Brigadier Sydney Kent was the secretary and their first report came out in August 1965. Their terms of reference were 'to make recommendations on the general programme of all races and stakes, with special attention to the top-class horses of all ages, the prestige races and the improvement of the thoroughbred'. Although the report has turned out to be immensely important to European racing, Lord Porchester must take the credit for galvanising the racing authorities into action. He went to the Jockey Club supremo, then General Randle Fielding, urging action on the report. The Stewards of the Jockey Club gave the go ahead and a committee headed by Lord Porchester with Peter Willett and Sidney Kent became the Race Planning committee. It issued its first report in 1967 and 131 races were adopted as Pattern races in Britain. There are now 292 Pattern races, an enormous increase on the original programme. The five main European countries participating (Britain was quickly joined by France and Ireland and Italy and Germany came in later) each have a member on the committee, which is currently chaired by Adrian Glazebrook of Ireland.

The method of deciding where races stand in the Pattern is to take the first four horses home, add up their official rankings and divide by four, so that the fourth home is just as important as the winner as far as the rating of the race is concerned. This undoubtedly worked well for some time but is under fire now as a shortage of good staying three-year-olds has led to small fields for the Derby trials in particular.

The Pattern has had a dramatic effect on the profitability of racecourses because there is a fixed minimum and maximum prize money for all Pattern levels. Some racecourses are being asked to fund a level of prize money which is unsustainable for them and the Pattern is divided very unevenly amongst Britain's main racecourses. The Mandarins of the Jockey Club, who gained no less than sixty-one Pattern races for 'Headquarters' or Newmarket, little realised what a strain they put on their own finances in the process. Ascot comes next with forty-one, followed by York with twenty-six. Newbury, a less profitable course with a poor average attendance, has to fund twenty-three, including a Group one. At the other end of the equation, Chester, with the third highest (and vying for second highest) average attendance of any flat racecourse, has only eight Pattern races and one of those has been demoted from Group three to Listed. Whereas, Newmarket is weighed down with Pattern races, Chester's finances have been enormously improved.

The Pattern is basically carried by the Jockey Club, whose courses have over seventy percent of the Pattern. If you take a rough guide that sponsors pay for one-third, they are carrying two-thirds of the seventy plus percent, a burden which few racecourses could possibly carry. Ascot, York and Goodwood, all very profitable courses, who plough their profits back into racing, account for much of the remainder, whilst Chester, desperate to put money into Pattern races, is unable to do so.

Racing owes a great debt to the Jockey Club. No commercial organisation could possibly behave the way the Club does and with one major flat course making a serious loss and none of the major flat courses making much profit they are very reliant on their two jump courses, Cheltenham and Aintree, which make most of the declared profit, with Cheltenham the most profitable course in Britain by some margin.

As I said earlier, the Pattern committee covers five countries, Britain, France, Ireland, Italy and Germany. Italy and Germany were allowed to join although a number of pundits, who follow the development of the Pattern, including myself, wonder whether it was a good decision. Italian racing is virtually bust and no British winners are being paid, the result being they are no longer getting other than Italian horses. Germany produces the odd very good racehorse but their Pattern races attract few British runners. Racing in Britain has never been at a higher level with immense interest in horses like Frankel and Sea the Stars and over the jumps, Sprinter Sacre, the best National Hunt horse I have ever seen. Racing in Ireland is also flourishing, although the crowds go to the jump meetings not the flat and, but for the immense wealth of Coolmore, Irish flat racing would have serious problems.

France, where betting revenue is ploughed back into racing, has no financial problems and is able to sail serenely on with enormous prize money at racing's disposal. Despite that, many courses are poorly attended. In Britain prize money at the lower end has never been poorer with the winner's prize at the smaller meetings barely meeting the owner's costs for the day. The gap between Pattern and non-Pattern is enormous and an injection of cash into the lower end is desperately needed.

Chapter 5

Robert Sangster

Robert Sangster became a great friend and our friendship never faltered at any point over the lengthy period between our first meeting in 1965 and his untimely death. We both started off as relatively small owners, having a good time on the racecourse and we had a great deal in common. The first race meeting we went to was to back a horse of Robert's, called New Lisceard, trained by Eric Cousins. During the journey to Chepstow, Robert said that the horse was a reluctant starter and that he would get a good position to see the start, put his hands in the air if he got a decent break and I was to put our bets on. None of my normal bookmakers were there and I had to settle for Sam Barnes of Crewe, who was sound enough but the word charisma would not enter a description of him. I talked sweetly with Sam for nine minutes before the hand went up and I put on a bet several times larger than normal. We never had a moment's worry.

Our two local meetings were Chester and Haydock and Robert had a fantastic waitress called Ginger, who used to keep us a table in the restaurants and bring us champagne. Robert and I both worked and played hard and saw more and more of each other until he made a poor decision to go to France. He was encouraged by his father, who wanted to regain control of his company but to leave a magnificent estate and lifestyle, where he was very happy, and to take his wife and children to a foreign country, where he couldn't speak the language, seemed to me the height of folly. Sadly, so it was and although I could not prove it, I'm sure it led directly to the break-up of his marriage. Robert became increasingly unsettled.

His marriage broke up on one of the most traumatic weekends I ever remember. Tim Kitson and I had first met at the same dinner party I met Robert, and Christine had become a good friend of Sally, his wife.

Tim and I had given a joint dinner party for about forty at our bridge club, the Portland. The next day Tim's wife, Sally, joined us and we set off for Malaga to stay with Robert and Chris at a palatial house they had rented. At Malaga airport we were met by two of Robert's then closest friends, Billy and Annie Hart, who were very emotional and told us the

Sangster marriage was over. Neither Tim nor I believed them, thinking alcohol had led to a lot of exaggeration. However, when we got to the villa it was obvious things were very tense. Robert and I escaped to the golf course, where we played with Sean Connery and Tim Vigors. At dinner I found myself next to Christine, who complained bitterly about Robert's hangers on (mainly bloodstock agents) and how unhappy the marriage was becoming. I told her all marriages went through rocky periods and she must stick it out, when suddenly Robert appeared from the other side of the table and told me not to give Christine advice – he had obviously overheard! The next day consisted of drinks, lunch, more golf and we had a good dinner at a nearby restaurant. Robert insisted we went on to the local night club, where we were joined by Tim Vigors and his German wife, Heidi. I remember having the longest dance of my life with Heidi, she must have been a phenomenal dancer, as I can't dance a step, but it is amazing what sufficient alcohol will do! We all went back to the villa where Robert went to his study and Tim and I decided to play a couple of games of Backgammon. We had nearly finished our game when Chris came to the top of the stairs and said to Robert, who appeared with a letter in his hand, 'Come to bed darling, it's very late.' Tim and I finished our game, said goodnight, and I went to my small room on the ground floor. I looked at my watch and it was exactly four-thirty.

I was woken up after seven by what I first thought was a pounding in my head, but it turned out to be Tim banging on the door. 'How can you sleep through this terrible drama?' he said. 'Robert and Chris are splitting up and you are to take Robert on your flight this morning.' I got dressed quickly and joined Robert and Tim in the drawing room. Robert looking a much better colour than Tim.

I don't remember much about the journey back, though Robert raved on about his girlfriend, Susan Peacock, the wife of the leader of the opposition in Australia, Andrew Peacock. She had written the letter Robert had dropped and Christine had picked up. Robert and I said goodbye at Heathrow, where he was coming back to the following day to fly to his new love in Australia.

In fact his stay in Australia turned out to be extremely expensive for me, as the following weekend a horse Robert and I shared won the Hialech Turf Cup at sixty-six to one, with neither of us there. I hadn't even been told it was running!

It was one of the bloodstock agents Christine so disliked, who gave me the news and also that there was an offer of a quarter of a million dollars for our horse but we had to make a decision before his next race at Woodbine in Canada a few days on. The agent said he couldn't get hold of Robert, who seemed to have disappeared, could I find him? I replied that I would take the entire responsibility as I knew Robert would be delighted by the sale but the agent told me he could only take instructions from Robert. As I knew Robert rang his secretary every week day morning I was not too worried and on Monday I rang his secretary, Miss Markey, to say that I urgently needed to speak to him. There was a long pause and Miss Markey finally said, 'For the first time ever Mr Sangster is not ringing me and I have not heard from him for some days.' I said, 'But Miss Markey you know where he is?' 'Yes Mr McAlpine but I am under strict instructions not to tell anybody.' I said, 'But I'm not anybody, I'm Bobby McAlpine, his great friend and I'm dealing with something which will benefit us both.' 'I have my instructions Mr Bobby.' I then said, 'Well let's play a little game Miss Markey.' I then mentioned two places which elicited little response, but when I said Hawaii, there was a sharp intake of breath and I knew I had hit the jackpot. We had just bought a travel agency run by John Slesinger so I rang him up and asked where a very rich and trendy young couple would go and stay. To his credit, John identified the correct hotel and without thinking it out I rang up and asked to speak to Mr Sangster. I described him and Susan as best I could but got the answer there is nobody of that name or description here. Andrew Peacock, the cuckolded leader of Australia's opposition, was far cleverer; he rang up the same hotel and said he must speak about a most important business matter but he had lost the name and described Robert and Susan very clearly. He was put straight through to their room and the voice the other end said, 'Robert Sangster here.' 'Andrew Peacock this end.' Game, Set and Match!

The inevitable happened, Lord Henham was unplaced at Woodbine and finished up as a down-market stallion in Port Elizabeth, South Africa – a sad end to the story.

Meanwhile the lovebirds returned to England and I and other close friends were all introduced to Susan.

The next event of note was the Derby, where I always went as Robert's guest. The old pre-war stand at Epsom was still in existence and my cousin's company, Sir Robert McAlpine, who had built it, had the good sense to pick the one decent large box, where they did a lot of entertaining. Robert had used all his influence to get a medium-sized table in the main dining room between Lord Howard de Walden and Prince Khalid Abdullah. Charles Benson, who had become a close friend of Robert's four years earlier, was also close to the Aga Khan and told us all that Blushing Groom was strongly fancied. He was also favourite and as a result neither Robert nor I had a large bet on his own horse, The Minstrel, who won the race under a fantastic ride from Lester Piggott and in a pulsating finish with Hotgrove, owned by my Chester chairman, Philip Leverhulme.

Nick Robinson, who had been responsible for my original introduction to Robert, and I watched the race from the Iron stand, a sectioned off part of the Grandstand. Thrilled with Robert's triumph, we decided to have a quiet drink in the Iron stand bar, where, to our horror, we found Christine Sangster and her friend Annie Hart. Both were in floods of tears and although we bought them the best champagne in the house, Christine was desolate. In the space of a few months, life had completely changed for her and not being able to celebrate with Robert was a dreadful blow. Had she known Susan insisted on going with Robert to meet the Queen, her grief would have been even greater.

Nick and I went back to Robert's table, where the celebration was in full swing and Charles, who had extracted himself from the Aga Khan, was busy organising the night's entertainment in the private room at Annabel's. The story was he simply changed the floral arrangements colours from the Aga Khan's to Robert's, though he always denied it. The party was a tremendous one with even the taciturn Lester getting fully animated.

Susan found herself the girlfriend of one of the most influential owners in the country. I had met John Magnier when I went to stay with Susan Francis (now Purcell), who was looking after a stud near Cashel. She said she had squared it with Vincent O'Brien's groundsman and we could land our company plane on a grass strip Vincent had converted into a runway. With great difficulty we finally found the runway and landed. No sooner had I given Susan a peck on the cheek than Vincent emerged out of the bushes. 'Fancy you calling in to see us, Bobby,' was his greeting, to my acute embarrassment. However an invitation to dinner followed, which saved a very expensive evening at the Cashel Palace. Susan was just driving into the entrance of Ballydoyle when a car swept down the drive and narrowly missed us. 'That was a recent boyfriend, John Magnier,' she said; 'now he has found Susan O'Brien I won't see him for dust.' We had a very enjoyable dinner and John arrived back with Vincent's eldest daughter and we all had a pleasant after-dinner drink.

Robert's alliance with John was to transform the top echelons of racehorse ownership. Up until then very rich international figures had bred and owned top-class racehorses knowing they were going to lose money and plenty of it. However Robert and John and one or two others who couldn't stand the pace, set out to make money by buying the very best animals with the object of making them into multi-million-pound stallions, and Coolmore was transformed, at considerable expense, into one of the greatest stud farms in the world. I well remember going there to give advice to Phonsie O'Brien about what fish to put in his pools.

The Minstrel went on to win the Irish Derby and the King George VI at Ascot, where another big celebration took place. He was then sold, for a small fortune at the time, to a syndicate headed by E.P. Taylor, a Canadian billionaire, who bought half of the thirty-six shares on offer. Although nobody then realised it, The Minstrel's sire, Northern Dancer, was to have more influence on breeding than any other of his era. Even more incredibly by the end of 1977's flat season Robert was to own an even higher-rated horse than The Minstrel.

Anybody who thought, in the middle of 1977 flat season, that the Sangster, Magnier, O'Brien syndicate would have such a horse, would have been thought totally mad, yet Alleged, also trained by Vincent O'Brien, ended the season with a higher *Timeform* rating than The Minstrel. Even more incredibly, Alleged was beaten, at odds on, in the St Leger by a great staying filly of her Majesty the Queen, Dunfermline. Alleged came to prominence in the Great Voltigeur Stakes, run at the York Ebor meeting, where he beat Hot Grove by ten lengths, giving him four pounds. Although beaten in the St Leger by Dunfermline, Alleged still started favourite for the Prix de l'Arc de Triomphe which he won comfortably with Dunfermline well behind in fourth place. Sadly the sale of The Minstrel meant he and Alleged were never to meet on the racecourse. As *Timeform* said at the end of 1977, a meeting of the two would have been worth going a long way to see. It is also worth mentioning that Alleged's defeat of Dunfermline in the 'Arc' proves what a difference an extra two furlongs makes between that race and the St Leger.

1977 was a momentous year for Robert and it also saw the second marriages of two of his closest friends, Charles Benson and Nick Robinson. His own took place in March of the following year and Susan, who had witnessed all his great triumphs on the racecourse the year before, became his bride.

I did not stay for the festivities over three days with Robert in his palatial Isle of Man house, The Nunnery, as I usually did but instead with Dudley Cunliffe Owen, who chaired the company which built the casino at the Palace Hotel, my company doing the work. I played golf with Robert the afternoon before and he was continuously looking at the sky, as the cloud base was very low and John Magnier, Vincent O'Brien and all the Irish were to fly in that afternoon. It was one of the most lucrative days on the golf course I have ever had playing Robert!

All was well and the Irish joined us for a large dinner party at the Palace Hotel, where Charles Benson, who made the speech, announced to the big contingent of Australian ladies present that there were two about-to-be-eligible bachelors present, the Earl of Suffolk and Bobby McAlpine.

Although I was trying to keep quiet about my marriage being on the rocks, the one Australian lady also staying with the Cunliffe Owens undoubtedly pricked up her ears. This was Nicky Spice, who had already had two marriages and was working for Di Hanbury, Dudley's sister, in an interior decorating business in Chobham, Surrey. Although the weekend passed innocently enough, the seeds were sown for the most traumatic and intense relationship that followed. It was with Nicky at my side that we went, first to the Guineas meeting and then to the Derby. We were at Robert's usual table and he had an outsider, Hawaiian Sound, deserted by Lester Piggott and trained by his other main trainer, Barry Hills – but he did manage to persuade Willie Shoemaker to come over from America to ride him. Shoemaker had ridden 7,000 winners, more than any at the time alive or dead, and in the Derby of 1978 he gave Hawaiian Sound the most wonderful ride, leading until the last strides and going under by only a head. Robert was naturally ecstatic and determined to have a celebration arranged at Annabel's the following Friday (the Derby was always on a Wednesday in those days). There were far fewer people than the previous year and although Nicky was at the Derby with me, I had promised Zandra Johnson I would take her to any Derby celebration that ensued and I kept my word. This resulted in my sitting well down the table between Zandra and Cindy Shoemaker, Willie's wife, who was as tall as Willie was short. Full of alcohol I boldly asked Cindy, late on, if it was difficult for a six-foot lady to cope with a tiny gentleman. Roaring with laughter, Cindy replied that when two people decide to do things together, nothing gets in their way!

At Royal Ascot both Robert and I stayed with Di and Toddy Hanbury, as we had for some years, and I went back to Nicky and virtually moved in with her after the meeting. We both went to stay with Robert and Susan a number of times in the Isle of Man and it was at one of those stays when I was talked into going to the Melbourne Cup by Susan and Nicky.

Despite the fact that I did an immense amount of long distance flying on business, I have never been a good air traveller, finding it very difficult to sleep, however comfortable the seats on the plane. Robert was the opposite, once telling me that one of his greatest enjoyments in life was to go first class from one part of the world to another, having had a wonderful dinner and then, after taking a couple of Mogodon (sleeping pills), waking up close to the destination.

We set off for Melbourne on Singapore Airlines, with one stop at Singapore, and were supposed to continue on to Melbourne in the same plane. The leg from London to Singapore went well, but the stopover in Singapore was delayed and the humidity didn't help. We were transferred to a different and much older plane and by the time we landed in Melbourne I was exhausted.

We were met by Nicky's parents, who were delightful, but we were booked into the Hilton Hotel as Sir Robert and Lady McAlpine, which may have amused Susan but certainly didn't do the same for anybody else. In fact it was my first experience of Susan's extraordinary behaviour, which was to increasingly annoy Robert in the forthcoming years.

It took me two days to revive sufficiently to enjoy all the festivities, which were in full swing. I had not realised quite how powerfully Robert was regarded in Australia. After all he had only become a leading owner in Britain very recently. But he was very much 'Mr Big' out there and Susan was revelling in it. Charles Benson was also in his element as Robert needed him at his side to write speeches and often speak for him as he was still a shy person. From my point of view there were aspects of the trip I thoroughly enjoyed. The racing was excellent and as an honoured guest of Robert, I was in a unique position. Two days I particularly remember at Melbourne Races were being taken by Nicky's father to the men only, prime stand and by the Chief Steward of the Australian Racing Board, who wanted me to see how much better stewarding was in Australia. I have to say I thought we were just as competent as they were.

The most incredible day took place the first Sunday when I was rung up by Susan the day before and told not to go at noon to Robert's suite with Nicky as we usually did because I was to accompany her to a lunch which I would enjoy a lot more than Robert's boring racing lunch and she had arranged for Nicky to spend the day with her parents. With some trepidation I went to the front entrance at 12.15 on the dot and Susan, in the passenger seat of a smart car, said, 'Meet Andrew Peacock, who is giving us a lift to Rupert Clarke's lunch party.' Andrew did the driving and Susan extracted some of the details of his recent romance with Shirley MacLaine. After quite a long drive, we reached the Clarke's vast mansion and an attendant dashed over to park the car. The one thing I was not going to do was walk in with Andrew and Susan, so I latched on to Derek Nimmo and his lovely wife and we walked a few yards behind them. There must have been three hundred people in the marquee and we were met by a wall of noise. Ten seconds later you could have heard a pin drop, Susan had certainly affected an incredible entrance!

When I managed to buttonhole Susan, I asked, 'Have you told Robert what is going on?' 'No,' she said, 'he is so wrapped up in his racing he doesn't mind what I do.' I literally marched her over to a phone and made her ring Robert, who had fortunately not left the Hilton for his lunch date.

I shudder to think how Susan had described me to her hosts because I was treated like royalty. Rupert Clarke was Australia's top banker and had taken over the Clydesdale Bank, where I and my family had banked all our lives. I was seated at the top table, next to Lady McMahon, the wife of the former Prime Minister. The high spot was Lady Clarke introducing the guest speaker, Derek Nimmo. She finished the introduction with a great sweep of her arm, which sent a beaker of Pimms he was drinking into his lap, ruining the Garrick tie he always wore. A seasoned trooper he quickly recovered!

Melbourne Cup day was amazing. The whole country literally stopped for it! We all started drinking, about ten in the morning, Australian champagne (in fact very light, good, fizzy, white wine). It says much for the drink that although we drank it non-stop until well into the evening, I did not have a hangover the next day. I watched the big race with Nicky and some English friends I had bumped into and shouted out, 'The favourite (owned by Robert) is lame.' I nearly got lynched by a group of locals but was proved absolutely correct when the horse pulled up after half a mile.

These were great days for Robert and Susan but they were not to last, as Susan's flamboyant behaviour and love of publicity increasingly got to Robert. The following year we went to the Guineas and Robert bought us all tickets for a charity lunch. To my surprise I found myself sitting next to Jerry Hall and her friend, David Bailey's wife. Jerry Hall wasn't remotely interested in me and my attempts at polite conversation were rebuffed to the point of rudeness. When we got up to get some cheese, Jeremy Hindley, who had been observing my lack of progress said, 'Let's change places, you're not getting anywhere.' 'With pleasure,' I replied. So he sat down and made his opening remarks to Jerry Hall. 'Will you not interrupt me when I am talking to my friend,' she replied, and turning to face Mrs Bailey she never addressed another word to Jeremy. I watched the scene with considerable satisfaction. When a few months later, the British press latched on to a romance between Robert and Jerry Hall and her estrangement with Mick Jagger, we were all agog. Jeremy was one of the first to ring me. 'Surely we aren't going to have that ghastly woman come into our lives?' was his opening remark. In fact a romantic liaison was set up in Los Angeles of all places. Robert set off with Charles at his side to go via Australia, where the pair sought Kerry Packer's advice and got told, 'Avoid the media at all costs.' Just a little late in the day! They spent four days in Los Angeles, with those of us in England waiting with baited breath for the outcome. Di Hanbury had gone to the Isle of Man, where she gave Susan the same advice as Kerry Packer had given her husband and literally stood over the phone, refusing to let Susan answer it.

The romance fizzled out. Robert came back with his tail between his legs. Susan's reward was to receive some very expensive jewellery and Di Hanbury got a contract to completely renovate the Nunnery. I often tried to get out of Charles exactly what happened in the four days but for once he was very reticent, replying he got much the best of it by latching on to Jerry Hall's sister. I don't think either of the principal men covered themselves with glory!

Robert's life settled back into its normal routine, with racing continuing to be successful and the policy of buying top-class colts to turn into stallions really paying dividends.

His description to me of how a sale of one top-class racehorse was conducted illustrates how well the Sangster, Magnier partnership was doing financially. John Magnier had rung up Robert to say he had an enormously wealthy American on the hook to buy their horse. At twenty-four hours' notice Robert went to America to meet the prospective owner. The meeting progressed to the point that the buyer was obviously prepared to pay twenty-five million dollars, which Robert felt was more than adequate and he gave Magnier a nudge to express approval and got a kick on the shins for his pains. 'You surely can't expect Robert Sangster to fly over at short notice to receive such a pathetic offer – he is a very busy man.' Eight million dollars later, the sale was agreed by all parties!

The one alarming element of the operation was how Robert's overdraft was going up. I was privileged to see both the valuations of the horses which were at the very top end of what they could have been sold for, and his overdraft which had gone to undreamed of heights. Although it was still below the valuations, it was not far enough, in my opinion, to feel comfortable. In fact I once asked Robert how he could sleep at night. 'Very well,' was the reply.

Robert's parties were legendary and the one he gave for Susan at The Nunnery in 1982 cost a small fortune. But the major expenditure was on the ever-expanding racing empire in England, Ireland and Australia.

His entourage however did not change greatly; he was very loyal to his friends and though inevitably he was surrounded by hangers on, a number of them became close friends as well. The two who were conspicuously at Robert's side were Charles Benson and Billy McDonald. Charles was undoubtedly indispensable to Robert and made no secret of the fact that he was perfectly happy to be called an 'arse crawler' if that kept his lifestyle going. But Billy was a more complex character and his entry into the drugs scene caused Robert considerable embarrassment. Whatever faults his inner circle had on the drink or smoking fronts, drugs were strictly not on our agenda.

One story typifies the problems. We had all become great fans of Barbados, which had started off when I rented Jeremy Hindley's house. His first house was in a village two miles from the shore but he had a beach hut, which, after I had rented the village house the first year, he completely rebuilt and was now a substantial holiday home. I had several friends staying, including Robert and Susan, but after one night Robert complained that the waves crashing into the shore had stopped him sleeping and moved into the popular hotel, Greensleeves. A few years later I was in fact staying with Nicky in Robert's Barbados house at James Harbour, adjacent to Sandy Lane. At the end of our stay Robert came up to me and said Susan has asked a freelance lady reporter who writes for the *News of the World* amongst other papers to come and write up our golf tournament and I just cannot have Billy meeting her. I have therefore divided our dinner party into two halves and have booked our favourite restaurant and we will be downstairs and you and Billy and several others will be upstairs. I agreed to this rather more easily than I should have. Dinner time arrived and Billy, who I sat next to myself, duly arrived. I then made the great mistake of appealing to Billy's better nature and telling him that as both of us were enjoying Robert's generous largesse it would do Billy no harm to accede to his wishes. The first course came and I talked to Billy through it but when the main course arrived I got distracted by the lady my other side and to my horror I realised Billy had gone. Knowing exactly what trouble I was in, I grabbed Nicky and left for a bar where we had drinks and coffee before going back to James Harbour. In fact what Billy had actually done, was to go downstairs where he said to the journalist sitting next to Robert, 'I hear you like writing about these.' He then unbuttoned his trousers and put a very intimate part of his anatomy on the table and said, 'What do you think of this one?'

The next day I was woken up by Robert's polished, Bajan butler who, without a hint of a smile, said, 'Mr Sangster would love to give you a drink at eleven in the bar.' I inwardly shuddered and thought immediately it would be like going to the headmaster's study. In fact Robert opened a bottle of Don Perignon and poured a large glass for both of us. He then started on a lengthy harangue on how I had let him down. At that point I saw, out of the window, a most unexpected sight, namely Billy on all fours crawling like a baby across the lawn (he was trying to get from his bedroom to the Kitson's where he thought he might get some sympathy). I couldn't help myself laughing and Robert immediately said, 'And what's more you think it is funny.' Realising I must not let Robert turn around and see Billy I straightened my face and absorbed the lengthy rocket, by which time Billy, not the most athletic of men, managed to reach the other side.

Robert with his heavy involvement in Irish racing and breeding was always going to be a likely target for the IRA and sure enough a demand came for a substantial amount of money or he would be murdered. He was naturally very worried and felt particularly vulnerable in the Isle of Man, where the Manx police took the threat very seriously. He was not helped by getting conflicting advice from his friends, some of whom thought he should pay up. Robert spent a few years under threat but in the end his financial adviser, accountant and great friend, Ken Paul, told him he must not pay, saying, 'The unpopularity in England will dwarf any benefits in Ireland.' Robert took his advice but it was years before he felt really safe. One time I came into contact with the problem was when Angela, who I had just married, and I accepted an invitation to stay in Ireland and go to Phoenix Park racecourse. We all had lunch in the main restaurant and then moved across to a large box to watch the racing. Robert and I walked across together with Angela, Vincent and Jacqueline O'Brien escorted by several policemen with guns at the ready. Robert sidled up to talk to me and I, who knew Robert was the target, tried to keep a yard or two between us. We reached the box where two police with large guns stood on guard. Robert did not leave the box for the rest of the day.

The purchase of Manton put further strain on his finances. Manton is a wonderful place off the main roads just west of Marlborough and when Robert installed Michael Dickenson as his main English flat trainer, there were a few others who wished they had been given the opportunity. Michael was right at the top of the tree as a National Hunt trainer and was keen to establish himself on the flat. He had trained for both Angela and myself, my best horse with him being Compton Lad, a good hunter chaser, who would probably have won the Foxhunters if he hadn't come down when in a clear lead three out. The next race was the famous Gold Cup, when Michael saddled the first five home!

Michael had enjoyed tremendous support from his parents and was used to being surrounded by friends and relatives. To be moved to the south of England was daunting enough but to be left in isolation without much communication from Robert and his advisers made his task ever more difficult. Nor was he given any proven horses and when he started having runners they were mostly two-year-olds. The first season was a disaster and the second was starting badly before Robert lost patience and asked Barry Hills to take his place. Barry had always wanted to train at Manton. Twice when we had gone to a meeting in the West of England he took me off the route back to look at Manton, which he always said was the finest place to train in the country. When Robert offered him the chance to train there he never hesitated, leaving his eldest son, John, to train in his Lambourn yard. Unfortunately he never bothered to get a proper contract, guaranteeing security of tenure and that would catch up with him when Robert put the estate on the market at the end of the eighties.

1984 was another significant year in Robert's life story, as it was the last year he was to be Britain's leading racehorse owner, an accolade he had won five times in the preceding eight years. The bursting through of billionaire Arab owners had completely changed the picture.

It was also the year he met the lady who was to become the third Mrs Sangster. Angela and I were at Chester races, late on in the season, when Robert introduced us to two ladies. 'This is a friend of ours from the Isle of Man and she has a friend in Cheshire, so I have given them a lift.' Not taken in for a moment, we all agreed to have a drink after racing as Robert was still stewarding and was a Steward at the meeting.

The press also got after the fact that Robert's marriage was in trouble and all doubt was ended by Melbourne Cup week, where it was arranged between Charles Benson and Robert that Robert would move out of his enormous house in Sydney, leaving Charles to console Susan as best he could, and Robert would move into an hotel. When they all went to Melbourne, Robert and Susan would take separate rooms and it must have been a very uncomfortable week, quite unlike the one I had been on a few years earlier. Susan hung on in the Isle of Man with her two daughters hoping that Robert would relent, but that was never going to happen and Robert embarked on a third marriage with the strikingly attractive Sue, who had had two husbands, both millionaires, previously. Whereas Robert's friends had been appalled at the breakup of his first marriage, a number were relieved to see the back of Susan. The exceptions were part of the racing fraternity who feared the new broom might look to a reduction of his massive racing interests. In this they were to be partially correct. Sue was far more streetwise than Susan and could see that Robert was spending far too much money, part of it unnecessarily. The first bit of Robert's empire to go was Vernair, the company that was flying Robert and his horses all over Europe. Whilst Sue was careful not to discourage Robert's love of racing she sought to save money where possible and he was no longer the soft touch to bloodstock agents he had been in the past. Moreover he began selling to the Arab princes some of the very best of his horses, much to the fury of some trainers. He had always recognised that the arrival of billionaire Arabs would raise the value of his bloodstock and now started to put it into full effect. In the years that followed there was only one sale he really regretted, the sale of Dr Devious. When Dr Devious won the Dewhurst at Newmarket, after Robert had sold him, Robert put on a brave face to the press, saying how delighted he was that the buyers had been so successful and got much praise the next day for his good sportsmanship. In fact he buttonholed me, took me to a back bar, ordered two bottles of champagne and said, 'Now I can tell you, who understands me so well, how I really feel!'

The one event where no expense was spared was Robert's fiftieth birthday, in the summer of 1986, where the party held, at the Nunnery, will never be forgotten by those who were at it. Guests came from all over the world and the cabaret was headed by Paul Anka, who flew from America with a backing group of over twenty musicians. There were two bands and the firework display put on, close to midnight, caused a major uproar in more ways than one. The local residents ringing Manx radio continuously with complaints. A local MP appeared at the gates in his pyjamas and questions were asked in the Manx parliament. The next day we were all given lunch in a marquee on the island's racecourse, where the Manx Derby took place, then worth ten thousand pounds to the winner and their richest race. The birthday boy duly won it and Robert, who was so enjoying himself, wanted to miss the presentation; Charles Benson and I almost had to use force to persuade him to attend.

Ten years later he was to have another memorable birthday party when he took all his guests by Eurostar to Paris. Two great dinners were organised, the second of which being the real party. As usual Charles Benson was to make the speech but whereas he was on his best behaviour at Robert's fiftieth, he had developed a technique in the intervening years of really savaging his host and I had suffered in a major way when Angela produced him to speak at my landmark birthday a couple of months earlier. He started off fairly mildly with Robert but was warming up on how all the children's wealth was vanishing and was about to embark on the Jerry Hall saga when a nearly comatose Robert suddenly woke up, grabbed the microphone out of Charles's hands and proceeded to make virtually the first speech I ever heard from his lungs. Charles was devastated and sulked for the rest of the weekend.

I suppose the best way to describe Robert's racing empire in the years following his last champion owners triumph in 1984 would be a slow decline as the Arabs gained a further and further grip on the prize money.

In 1992 he still had a good year and won the 2000 Guineas, the Juddmonte International, the Champion Stakes and the Irish 2000 Guineas, all with Rodrigo de Tiano, and had he not sold Dr Devious he might well have finished in second place in the owners prize money table. As it was and despite winning four top Group races that included an English and Irish classic, he only finished in sixth place, behind five Arab owners, Sheikh Mohammed coming first by a distance.

A year later it was a very different story, Robert finishing twenty-fifth in terms of prize money won, behind ten Arab owners, the Aga Khan and three O'Brien owners named individually Sue Magnier, J Smith and Michael Tabor. One big consolation was that Sadler's Wells came top of the winning sires list and indeed the income from this great sire was to help Robert through his remaining years.

His owners listing is interesting with sixty-five horses down for the Northern Hemisphere and thirty-two for the Southern, i.e. Australia, where his youngest son, Adam, was looking after them and where he was still a very big name. Interestingly he listed twenty-four trainers for his ninety-seven horses. He still had a very large stud with one hundred and thirty-three broodmares dotted around the world.

Robert was also selling some of his best horses, including fillies. I well remember an agitated Barry Hills when Robert sold a top filly out of the stable to Sheikh Mohammed despite Barry having got together two or three of his owners to put up the same amount of money. I, amongst others, talked to Robert but he would not budge and I suppose the Sheikh had become too important to him to risk offending him.

Robert's greatest mistake though was undoubtedly his failure to join the Magnier, McManus, Tabor, Lewis syndicate, who, under the guidance of Joe Lewis, a genius in his field, made a fortune investing on overseas currency exchanges. It changed the syndicate from rich to immensely rich and from then on Robert, once the great financier of the Magnier, O'Brien, Sangster partnership got increasingly left behind. Nowhere was this more marked than in Barbados, the playground of all the group and where Robert became a full resident after leaving the Isle of Man. The high spot of the post Christmas holiday month of January was a pro/am golf tournament, initially mainly sponsored by

Robert and assisted by the ever-at-his-side Charles Benson, and Sally, the wife of one of his English trainers, Jeremy Hindley, who also played in the tournament.

The pros were very much the leading British professionals of the day and although they were big names it was the amateurs who really decided the outcome. My most memorable moment was the draw on the eve of day four, the last of the tournament, when Charles Benson had got Albert Finney to do the draw for partners. Without Robert's knowledge Charles had decided that Robert should have a top amateur, who was playing better than his handicap. Albert was given a piece of paper and the sight of him trying to regurgitate it had those of us who understood what was going on in hysterics with laughter.

As the Irish contingent grew richer, so the balance of the tournament began to change and John Magnier, originally the junior partner, became much more dominant. I should have won the tournament my last year, when I had a top Ryder Cup pro and two amateurs including Archie Sterling, in a team of four. We had not done particularly well the first three days nor did the first eight of nine holes give much encouragement. The rules had been changed and all four had to complete a score on the final difficult hole, where it was easy to go out of bounds. We all drove well and Archie Sterling, who had not scored a point until then, got an Eagle and the other amateur a Birdie. The pro had a straightforward putt for an Eagle but the ball went half into the hole and hit a little too hard finished eighteen inches away. Furious with himself he tried an angry backflip and missed the return. I also missed a short putt for a Birdie and we all assumed we had thrown away any chance of being in the top four. In fact, those who looked like winning got into all sorts of trouble and I finished second, one stroke behind. Either my short putt or the pro's eighteen inch one would have caused a play off and as the winner had cancer and was exhausted I would almost certainly have won that.

Barry Hills and I had shared a house for quite a few years but we decided to try Cape Town for our holiday, where Dick Bonnycastle joined us at a nice house in Constantia. The three of us did go back for one year when Sandy Lane was closed for reconstruction having been bought by J.P. McManus and others of the Magnier team. J.P., a most generous man, knowing Robert would hate the dust and noise, had made him an offer well above market price but Robert stubbornly refused to take it and it was not until after his death that J.P. stepped in and bought if off his children.

We had been recommended to the next expensive hotel after Sandy Lane by one of Barry's owners; it was incredibly expensive and the restaurants even more so. The influx of all the multi-millionaires had a dramatic impact on pricing and the island was far removed from the unspoilt retreat I had first started off holidaying on.

Robert adored the place and I often wondered whether this led to the breakup of his third marriage, which came as a great surprise to even his closest friends like myself. He and Sue remained great friends with the odd row over alimony and when Charles Benson died, after a long battle with cancer, the wake was held in her flat. I got a lift to it with Nigel Dempster, who had been given the use of a chauffeur-driven car by the *Daily Mail* as he also was starting a major degenerative illness. We reached Sue's sumptuous flat and Nigel said, 'I know she got a good payoff but I didn't realise it was this good.' Robert took a group of us to lunch and another chapter of his life story had closed.

He also cut down the number of race meetings he attended, mainly because his days in England were rationed. We usually first met at Newmarket, either the Craven meeting or the Guineas, which I always went to in the days the 1000 Guineas was on a Thursday. Robert would always stay with me for the Chester May festival and there was one hilarious year when I had bought Swettenham Hall from him and he came to stay with Angela and myself there. The first night after an alcoholic day at the races and a good dinner, he wandered, totally disorientated and stark naked, into our bedroom (which used to be his) and I had to lead him to the main spare bathroom.

Although I had by this time inherited family money, Robert, whose father had made over to him the Vernon Pool company, was way ahead of me on that front and although Eric Cousins was a very successful country trainer, he was looking for more leading ones and started having horses with Barry Hills and then Vincent O'Brien, where he teamed up with John Magnier, Vincent's son-in-law.

After I had bought Tilstone he always stayed with me for Chester. Then at Epsom, having one of the prize tables he did not want to buy an expensive box and anyway he gave up going to the Derby and went to his son's sports day instead. However he did buy one of the prize boxes at Ascot and I always spent the first day in it and then came after lunch on the other days. Joan Collins was the first celebrity to come to the box, usually on the second day because her then boyfriend played in the Barbados golf tournament. She was followed by Anthony Andrews, Nigel Havers and Ronnie Wood, who also became regulars.

It was in the last days of the box, before the new stand was built, that I had my most dramatic moment in it. My wife had decided she had had enough of Ascot and I was on my own; I had driven down from Cheshire and arrived early, having stopped for two cups of coffee on route. Angela was trying to keep my weight down and I had had no breakfast. It was also a sweltering hot day and I was wearing my heaviest morning coat and waistcoat. I was the first into the box and eventually Tim Kitson arrived and started talking about the Lords and Commons bridge team, which toured Europe. The next thing I knew I was lying flat on my back with Bill Gredley pouring water over my face and John Gosden saying he had called the course doctor, who arrived a couple of minutes later. He took my blood pressure, which he said was too low and then said I would have tests in the first aid room. He refused to let me walk and the paramedics arrived with a stretcher and I was wielded out of the box through a crowd of people, looking curiously, to the first aid room, which was fortunately about the best in the country. I was given tests for heart and stroke problems but they could find nothing wrong with me and I returned to the box, where I was greeted with total amazement, nobody expected me to return. Robert admitted later that he thought I was a 'goner' and Tim Kitson was trying to ring my family to tell them I had a serious seizure, probably a major stroke, and Nigel Dempster, at whose feet I had passed out, was looking very pensive. I did ask Sally Hindley to make sure Dempster didn't print anything and she said she had already asked him to keep quiet. I then sat down and had a large plate of food. The day ended on an hilarious note with Nigel Havers pretending to take my blood pressure and giving me advice to drink plenty of water. 'But you are not a doctor,' I said. 'No, but I have played so many I know more than most of them,' he replied.

I went back to William Barlow's, where I was staying and the following morning the papers arrived. As soon as William opened the *Daily Mail* I knew I was in trouble, being Nigel Dempster's lead story, with for once a good photograph of me in a morning coat at a happier Ascot, and some nonsense about my being tougher than the reinforced concrete I was used to.

In fact when I went to my G.P. and asked for a check-up, he was to tell me I had a simple faint due to dehydration, which he said would look terrifying to other people. He gave me some excellent advice: never go without breakfast, the most important meal of the day, and if you must drink a lot of coffee, drink plenty of water as well. I didn't tell him Nigel Havers had already given me that advice!

Although Robert was never to see the new stand, his old box is still there next to one now rented by the Jockey Club as its 'drinks' box for members and guests after lunch.

Whereas everybody knew some time ahead that Charles Benson was dying, nobody dreamt that a couple of years later Robert would go the same way. The year before he had come to Chester as usual and asked me if I would go and stay with him in Spain, where he had bought a house near Valderama, which was where a lot of friends had gathered. When I arrived he was not there and there appeared to be little security as I walked through an open front door and helped myself to a cold beer from the fridge. I sat down in the drawing room and Robert arrived with two friends from the early Irish days, Mick O'Toole and Phonsie O'Brien. We played golf every day in the heat of the day which, though not as intense as July or August, was still considerable. He seemed healthier and fitter than he had been for some time and said he had never felt better. We had a simply wonderful week and had splendid dinners at good, local restaurants and frequent talks about life in general. He had introduced me to his young Australian girlfriend, who had been hidden away at his daughter, Kate's, wedding, and who seemed nice and very attractive. When I suggested she would make an excellent companion, he told me he would not commit to her and was hoping to get back with Sue. How or if this progressed I was not to know because I was never to have a proper conversation with him again.

We never saw much of each other anyway during the winter because he hardly came to England and I spent the last week of January and the first two of February with Barry and Penny Hills and Dick Bonnycastle in Cape Town. We returned to hear the devastating news that Robert had collapsed on the plane back to England, on the last day of the Barbados golf tournament. He had been rushed into hospital and had a major operation. When I rang Guy, his eldest son, he told me Robert was still in intensive care but that he would ring me as soon as his father was able to take phone calls. A couple of days later he rang me to say that Robert was much better and would love to talk to me. I also arranged to go to London to see him. However, when I rang Robert he was his old jokey self, 'I went up to the Pearly Gates, St Peter took one look at me and sent me down again; I am absolutely fine. Book me in for Chester and don't worry about me.' Reassured I cancelled my immediate visit to London, which Robert said didn't suit him and arranged to go up the next week. However one of the elder boys, Guy or Ben, rang me to say that Robert had pancreatic cancer and was worse again. I also talked to Sue, who said she was preparing the younger children for the worst. When I arrived for my visit I was met by a grim faced Ben, who told me Robert was in a coma and I might prefer to remember him as he was. He died the next day.

The funeral drew a massive number of friends and I was terrified I might be asked to do an address but the family had the good sense to ask my cricketing friend, Colin Ingleby MacKenzie, the best public speaker around, and he really rose to the occasion. I was to attend Colin's memorial a year later at St Paul's Cathedral. Robert's wake was equally memorable in a large hotel with all his pictures and trophies on display. Angela and I were placed in the front row of the church as was John Magnier, who some people, quite wrongly, thought had fallen out with Robert. All went well until Guy put Robert's young, Australian girlfriend next to me; she was weeping and floods of tears were coursing down her cheeks. Never at my best in these situations, I was rescued by the arrival of Wendy Cousins, who had been Robert's director of racing, the other side of her, who said, 'Now my dear we must all pull ourselves together for Robert's sake.' And thankfully the tears subsided until Hughie de Berg sang a lament towards the end of the service.

Robert had a great ability to enjoy life and a temperament to cope both with the major successes and the setbacks that were part of it. He had a first-class brain and would almost certainly have massively increased the family fortune in business if he had not been so bitten by the racing scene. Although surrounded by people who stood to gain financially from him, he learnt to cope with their adulation and was well aware of the faults of the main two, Charles Benson and Billy McDonald, who were both important in maintaining his lifestyle. He also stuck with his old friends, myself, Tim Kitson and Nick Robinson in particular. He was, in short, one of the most genuine people I have ever come across.

Chapter 6

The Jockey Club

When I was elected a member of the Jockey Club in June 1975, it was one of the most exciting events of my life. Philip Leverhulme, who gave me the good news, was plainly delighted that somebody he was anxious to promote in racing was going to join the Club. He himself had just retired as Senior Steward, having done an excellent job during his tenure and started a reforming process which Lord Howard de Walden accelerated in a major way in his period of office, particularly in regard to allowing women to become trainers and jockeys. He had a large agenda, knew exactly what he wanted to do and achieved much needed and substantial reforms. What I had not realised and only recently discovered was that it was his third period of office, so he did have some practice.

Although the Club officially gives the year it dates back to as 1750, the club's historians believe it could have been even earlier. What nobody doubted was that consistent rules were needed and an authority to whom appeals could be made and whose decision was final. Whilst there were hundreds of courses in existence, most were dependent on local aristocrats to promote racing and apply rules as they saw fit.

The first recognised maker of rules was Charles II, but after his death there were major problems. John Cheney, who published a yearly calendar and review of racing, summarised the state of the turf in his calendar of 1732 as follows: 'The diversion of horse racing is advanced to such a height as to render the practice of it intimate and familiar to every part of the Kingdom; notwithstanding which the accidents incident to these affairs are so numerous, the conditions of running so various and different; the articles or advertisement or both, so often capable of counter construction, the methods of deciding bets in particular cases, known to so few, and with such reluctance submitted to by many, who are well acquainted with them, that these affairs are frequently attended with disputes and contentions too many of which proceed to expensive law suits, that terminate not, but with the additional evil of leaving behind them impressions of resentment, between persons concerned.'

Nineteen years later, in 1751, his calendar had a small announcement that on 1st April 1752, there was to be run a contribution free plate, the horses the property of the noblemen and gentlemen belonging to the Jockey Club at the Star and Garter in Pall Mall.

We do not know who these members were but in 1752 they got land to build a Coffee Room at Newmarket. They soon made their influence felt and in 1757 a dispute at The Curragh was referred to the Jockey Club in Newmarket. The following year Heber published the first general order of the Jockey Club. In 1762 a second order was published, in which 19 peers and gentlemen, all members, registered colours they agreed to use consistently.

The Jockey Club's early attempts to seek authority over horse racing centred on Newmarket, where its influence was very strong but it was long into the future before they had control over the sport in the rest of Britain. In 1770 they issued a notice in the Calendar: 'Chester Races, in order to save Mr Quick, Mr Castle or any of the Ascot confederacy the trouble and expense of training they are desired to take notice that none of their horses will be allowed to run in any of the plates (and there followed the list of local plates), nor will Thomas Dunn be permitted to ride.'

The Club was certainly trying.

Control required records to be accurately kept and communicated and there were several who followed John Cheney in this respect. However, in 1773 the Jockey Club authorised the new keeper of the Match Book, James Wetherby, to publish a calendar; thus started an association which has lasted to this day. The Weatherby family became the support team behind the club and amazingly, 224 years later, a descendant of James Weatherby is now Senior Steward of the Club.

In 1791, James Weatherby published his first volume of a stud book, *Introduction to a General Stud Book* and, in 1800, the first supplement was published and, in 1808, what purported to be a final one.

The Jockey Club's control over racing gradually increased as the nineteenth century unfolded and they were greatly helped by one of the true legends of the turf, Admiral Rous. He became a Steward of the Jockey Club and started to handicap horses. In 1850 the club was about to appoint a public handicapper but Rous opposed the appointment and took over the job himself, which he kept until his death. By 1860 he was effectively a dictator over the turf and his knowledge of the rules brought to him disputes from all over the country. He died at the age of 82 in 1877 and his influence in promoting the Jockey Club as the sole authority over racing was immense. Just before his death he headed the three Stewards, Lord Falmouth and Mr Chaplin being the other two. There were nineteen other members, including two princes.

A typical Jockey Club notice read as follows: 'Complaints having been made to the Stewards of the Jockey Club by William Hamshaw on behalf of his son, Wm Hamshaw, an apprentice, against Mr T Stevens of Chilton (his master) and his sons, that he had been frequently ordered by Mr T Stevens Junior, to pull or prevent horses in their stable from winning. The Stewards (Lord Calthorpe sitting for Admiral Rous) have diligently enquired into all the circumstance of the case, having heard the evidence they are of the opinion that the gravest suspicion attaches to Mr T Stevens, W G Stevens and with regard to T Stevens junior. They have no alternative but to inflict the severest penalties. They therefore decide that Mr T Stevens junior be warned off Newmarket Heath and that no horses under his care are allowed to run in any race or at any meeting where the rules of racing, as established at Newmarket, are in force.'

The calendar of 1875:

I Thomas Smith, tender my humble apologies to Sir George Chetaugh and the gentlemen of the Jockey Club and unhesitatingly withdraw the unwarranted and insolent expressions which I made as of regarding the running of Tangible at Sandown Park.

Ripon: The Stewards of this meeting, having reported Shead, the jockey, to the Stewards of the Jockey Club for not trying to win on Rock Rose in the Great St Winifred's Handicap, taking into consideration his previous good character, suspended him from riding until the end of the year only.

1896 had a notice that the following were elected members of the Club:

The Earl of Cawder

Hon. W Gerard

Viscount Folkstone

Duke of Westminster

And a meeting was headed:

H.R.H. Prince of Wales

Sir J Astley (in the chair)

And finished:

The Senior Steward nominated his successor, who was unanimously approved by the meeting.

Voting was apparently a very important part of the proceedings and in 1879 an amendment to the rules was narrowly carried, 21 for and 18 against.

They fared much better a century later with Edward, Prince of Wales (later King Edward VII). He started modestly and cheaply but gradually increased his string and started the Sandringham Stud in 1885. As noted in Chapter 1, he won the Derby of 1896 with Persimmon and received one of the greatest receptions ever witnessed on a racecourse. He won the Triple Crown in 1900 and the Derby again as King in 1909. He is the only member of the Royal family to have taken an active part in meetings of the Club and although proceedings were not then taken verbatim, his influence must have been considerable.

In 1883 the Jockey Club announced that no new courses would be recognised unless they met strict standards regarding fencing and general enclosure. A lot of the smaller courses could not meet the standards and closed down. As the century progressed rules continued to develop and the Club's authority grew, and by the end of the century it was virtually absolute.

The Racing Calendar meticulously recorded all races under Grand National Hunt rules. When a meeting had races under Jockey Club rules they were referred to as other races under the rules of racing. The edition for the 1881/82 season had as their last entry, the Derby summer meeting, the Meynell plate of 100 sovereigns for hunters, the other races were under the rules of racing. Bangor had only one meeting in April with ten races, starting with the Grand Wynnstay Steeplechase of 100 sovereigns. Ludlow Club also had one meeting but it lasted for two days. Sandown Park had eight meetings, the first in September had two races for hunters, one two miles on the flat and a selling race on the flat also two miles. The second meeting had one hurdle race, the third three steeplechases, three hurdles and one flat race on the first day and the second day had six races, two flat, two hurdles and two chases. The third day had two chases and four hurdles. Whereas at Bangor and Ludlow only amateurs rode, Sandown was open to professionals in most races. Manchester had five meetings and Croydon, where Queen Elizabeth I went racing, seven. Ireland is also recorded with forty-six courses of which Ballydoyle with five meetings had easily the most. Kempton Park had eight meetings.

The racing calendar also stated that a special general meeting of the committee held at Weatherbys' office, 6 Old Burlington Street, London, on July 23rd and at their office at Goodwood on August 3rd, the revised rules of steeple chasing as submitted by the committee appointed for the purpose, it was resolved that the following rules should come into operation on the first day of September 1897 and that all former rules be repealed on and from that day. In other words Weatherbys, on behalf of the Jockey Club and Grand National Committee, had got a firm grip on proceedings. The Grand National Committee numbered thirty-six of which eleven were peers, including one Duke (Hamilton).

The Stewards for the year were five, headed by Captain Coventry who had under him two peers and two retired Colonels.

The twentieth century was to be a period of enormous change for the Club, mainly at the end of it. When I was elected a member in 1975, Christopher Hill, writing about the Club, said the exclusiveness and autocracy has been widely commented on but it was also in its own way democratic. The Club was small with only about 57 members, 6 of them honorary, just before the amalgamation with the National Hunt Committee and the business was straightforward enough for all important issues to be presented to the members at general meetings, of which there were then 11 a year. If the Stewards sensed that the feeling of the meeting was against a proposal they would withdraw it. Now, with only 6 meetings a year, the greatly increased membership (115 in 1987 and 11 honorary and about 30 more now), the increased complexity and volume of business, and the growth of the committee system, far more work is left to the Stewards and the committees, so that the general meetings have become less important. It is worth pausing here because I believe Christopher Hill was very accurate in his assessment.

When I joined the Club, I was very surprised by its composition, and particularly by its lack of a method to elect its senior players, i.e. the Senior Steward and the other Stewards. Whilst they had enormous power, there seemed no recognised method of electing them. I had been brought up on Trade Federations and golf and cricket clubs, all of whom in their different ways had a recognised method of electing their leader or leaders.

Early on in my Jockey Club career I made a great error, which was to haunt me afterwards. There was a debate on Stewarding, which was a subject I was particularly interested in and, used to the cut and thrust of federation meetings, I started to argue with Julian Richmond-Watson's father, who was leading for the Stewards. What neither I nor the Jockey Club members realised was that my marriage was under strain and I was, frankly, not my normal self. Lord Howard took a dim view and my career in the Club went backwards from then on.

I was, I hope, intelligent enough to realise I had blotted my copybook in a major way but even I was not prepared for the enormity my ill-judged words had caused with the establishment.

There was one slightly amusing sequel: I was summoned by Uncle Robin to have lunch in his Park Street house. I had assumed that there was only one subject he could be about to berate me on, as I knew he read the Jockey Club minutes, where my words were down verbatim. I duly turned up and Robin, who was only to live a couple of years more, brought out a wonderful bottle of champagne and we proceeded to drink it. He, like me, was a great lover of champagne, his favourite drink. I waited for the rocket to come but what he had to say was totally unexpected, namely that he was crippled by arthritis and that my other uncle, Edwin, was too busy to attend the meetings. He then said that I had missed the last two meetings (I was keeping well away deliberately). When I got a chance to reply, I told him I felt I had made a complete fool of myself in the Stewarding debate and to my amazement he said he thought I had done rather well and that I should make a point of attending all the meetings as he and Edwin could no longer do so. I replied that I would do his bidding if he could answer one question, and when he agreed, I asked him how he thought the Senior Steward got elected? I can still see the look of bewilderment on his face and after a long pause, he replied, 'I haven't the slightest idea!' We went into lunch, where the wine was excellent and no more was said. I did not attend all the meetings as requested!

I have always said my first Senior Steward, Lord Howard, was the best of my time. He did have plenty of confidence after two previous spells as supremo, knew exactly what he wanted to do and proceeded to set about achieving all his goals. Christopher Hill is very complimentary in his book, *Horse Power*, about my racing mentor, Philip Leverhulme, who he described as a 'liberalising Senior Steward, who led the Club into a sustained period of adaption and modernisation, which continues to the present day' (Hill was writing this in 1987).

The next liberalising Senior Steward to confront major decisions was Stoker Hartington, now the Duke of Devonshire. He was faced with the problem that governments and particularly Labour governments, were not going to have serious discussions with a body which was unelected and had, perhaps unfairly, got the reputation of being autocratic and 'old school'. Christopher Hill described it at the end of his book as 'an extraordinary body, self elected, with many members who are rich and influential in other fields than racing. It has retained its power because it has had the wit to share and because its members publicly expressed attitudes have so changed that it is widely seen as genuinely less autocratic than in the past. According to where one stands politically, it is either a happy example of tradition at work or a disastrous comment on the current state of English society – and this is the body which is leading racing into the 1990s and towards the twenty-first century.'

I should say that although I was still regarded with suspicion by some diehard members of the establishment, my relationship with a number of leading members of the Club was good and perhaps my spell of racecourse management, as chairman of Chester and Bangor-on-Dee and as the first director of Aintree appointed by Peter Daresbury when he became chairman, stood me in good stead. The Jockey Club member who saved me from oblivion was Louis Freedman, the father of Philip Freedman, later chairman of the TBA.

I had got to know Louis well through his friendship with Brian Jenks, my old friend from Shropshire days, who was thoroughly enjoying the Jockey Club but took no part in any decision making and never spoke at meetings. Louis was quite different and had become a really influential member. One day he approached me and said that it was ridiculous I was not taking a greater part in the running of the Club and that it was high time I was on a committee. I told him that I had blotted my copybook in my early days in the Club but he said he thought I was greatly exaggerating the problem and there was no reason why I should not progress and that he was going to do something about it. I did not see Louis for a few months after that and when I did he was quite subdued and admitted that I was regarded as a difficult member and that one member of the establishment was particularly antagonistic. Nevertheless, he was going to press on as he thought I was being treated very unfairly. To my amazement, he succeeded and I was appointed to the Finance Committee, chaired by Charles Cadogan, the other members being Christopher Spence and 'Wenty' Allendale.

This was the first committee I was on since the Licensing Committee. I have to say I enjoyed this committee immensely. There were some highly interesting debates and we spent one memorable day at Weatherbys' Wellingborough offices, where we were shown the new computer set up and very well looked after. I shall always be grateful to Louis for achieving the impossible and getting me briefly near the centre of things. Another happy memory is that after our meetings we had lunch in the small Jockey Club dining room with the Stewards and other guests. The cook was my near, Cheshire, neighbour, Jennifer Rae, and she was to marry Charles Cadogan after my spell on the committee finished. Sadly the marriage did not last very long but both are now happily married to other people.

No account of the Jockey Club in the twentieth century could leave out the feud between the Club and Lord Wigg. They simply loathed each other. Strangely, Lord Wigg had his horses with my great friend and neighbour, Doug Francis. As Doug's other owners were mainly establishment figures including Anne, Duchess of Westminster, it was quite a feat on Doug's part to get on so well with everybody and he even persuaded me to buy one of Lord Wigg's horses, Fortition, who won a race or two but was no star. There is no doubt Lord Wigg did much for racing and Christopher Hill , writing in 1987, was well aware of this. He listed a number of Wigg's achievements, which included getting the criteria for the fixture list, which at the time provided for two fixtures a day, with quarter of an hour intervals between racing, so that punters could spend an afternoon in betting shops without getting bored. Another achievement was the success of his scheme to acquire United Racecourses, the owners of Epsom and Sandown and later Kempton. It is worth noting that Kempton was only offered by David Robinson to the Levy Board for a moderate sum, because he had been refused planning permission. Some other large courses were not so lucky!

Strangely, in his last letter to *The Times*, in 1982, Lord Wigg complimented the Jockey Club on its administration of the Rules of Racing but he concluded that racing was hopelessly addicted to subsidy and this had come about because the Club 'has maintained positions which have enabled it to exercise decisive power without regard to the economic consequences'.

Hill also tried to analyse Wigg's motives: 'It is true that although he became an officer himself, he disliked the officer class. He thought it morally wrong that racing should be run by a private club, so exclusive that it cut itself off from ninety-five percent of the available pool of talent.' I would certainly defend the Club on this; in my time they made a great effort to elect all those who would be useful to racing. My comment would be that having elected them in some cases they did not make sufficient use of them – mainly because only a small number could reach the top of the Club.

Stoker Hartington's spell as Senior Steward was the most eventful since Lord Howard. He had the view, rightly in my opinion, that the Club would not get anywhere talking to government and that a body needed to be created which embraced the mainstream needed to run racing where the Jockey Club would be in a minority but would still keep the administration of racing, which it had managed for nearly three centuries. He had a competent chief executive in Christopher Haines, who was ideally suited to assist him bringing in a revolution in Jockey Club history but one which was amply justified by the political situation of the day.

I will never forget the day he brought his proposals before the Jockey Club, as it was two days after the false start fiasco at Aintree, when the race had to be abandoned. Peter Daresbury was going on a skiing holiday, so I was the only Aintree board member attending the meeting.

I got a message to go straight to the Senior Steward's office as soon as I got to the meeting and a harrassed Lord Hartington obviously needed the Aintree fiasco like a hole in the head. He asked me my views and I said that I would have to blame the starter (a Jockey Club employee), who had lost control. Although he plainly didn't like my reply, he said I was to answer all the questions and I went to the meeting expecting a barrage of them. In the event there was not a single question and Stoker was able to get across his proposition for the new body, which became the British Horseracing Authority.

What he could not have foreseen was that his chief executive, Christopher Haines, lost out to Sir Tristam Ricketts for the post as chief executive of the new body, the chairman being the supremo. Haines was allowed to leave the Jockey Club almost unnoticed by its members and the media. Yet in my opinion the Club were very remiss in not persuading him to stay.

It was a number of years later that Julian Richmond-Watson appointed the current chief executive, Simon Bazalgette. Bazalgette was in most ways an excellent appointment. He had good connections with the media and a fresh modern outlook. His problem was he had little racecourse experience and this had led to the Club trying to centralise the management of racecourses, whereas, in my opinion, the most successful racecourses have been those where partnerships are formed between the chairman and chief executive over a lengthy period.

I was among a number of members led by Tim Holland Martin who disagreed with the decision to give away our administration functions; there seemed no great pressure to do so. It would have been interesting to have seen a vote taken. All water under the bridge now.

The Club has done two immensely important things for the good of racing. It has rescued a number of courses whose futures were uncertain and in one case, Aintree, which seemed certain to close down. It is ironic that the future was so bleak for the two great National Hunt courses, which now make up most of the profit that Jockey Club Racecourses declare.

It has also taken the burden of over 70% of the Pattern. Without the Club's involvement, it would have been impossible for the Pattern to be kept at anything like the current level.

For over two-and-a-half centuries the Jockey Club has ruled over the sport of Horseracing and all my research would indicate that on the whole it has done a good job. One frequent criticism is that they should have moved to get similar benefits to France, with a tote monopoly, but there was little appetite to do away with bookmakers at the time. Another was that the Club elected too many members of the aristocracy with the implication that many were not too bright either. Nevertheless, over the centuries some dedicated and far from brainless men devoted a large part of their lives to the sport, which is flourishing today.

What now for the Club? There is no doubt that the loss of its administration functions has left it in a very different position to any other time in its history. It still has great influence but its chief role is now the running of its fifteen racecourses, over half of them the most important in the land.

Is it doing a good job with racecourses? I would have to give a yes, and I suspect those at the top of the Club are convinced the answer is a resounding one. I personally would like to see the courses make more money to plough back into racing, although I am well aware the reason the profits are so low are largely down to the amount of the Pattern the Club is carrying. There seems to me, no reason why the club does not release a few Pattern races to the major independents who would welcome taking them on. The greatest problem is Newmarket, where racegoers are just not turning up in large numbers and there is too great a dependence for profit on Cheltenham and to a lesser extent, Aintree. A wipe-out of either the Cheltenham Festival or the Grand National meeting would cause great problems.

It is after all that has been said a great Club and I am sure I am speaking for most racegoers who would wish it well and thank it for the great contribution it is still making to the racing industry. I am certainly very proud to have been a member for so long and have nothing but affection for the Club and its wonderful history.

Chapter 7

Jockeys

This chapter is on the five greatest flat jockeys and the undoubted greatest National Hunt jockey to grace the British turf. There is one American, Steve Cauthen and for those who think I am biased I can only refer you to a fine judge, Peter Scudamore, who selected the same jockeys recently in an article for a national newspaper.

The first of the flat, **Fred Archer**, totally dominated the racing scene in the short period of his career. The second of thirteen children, his father had won the Grand National in 1858 and his mother was the daughter of the proprietor of the Kings Arms at Prestbury. Both father and son were keen followers of the Cotswold Hunt and it was there that Fred, a small child, caught the eye of the La Terriere brothers, two stalwarts of the hunt and very well connected. In fact their descendant, Ian Sales de La Terriere was the best Etonian Squash and Racquets player of his era and I was unfortunate to come up against him at the age of fifteen in the first round of the Public School Racquets competition. I was to get my revenge many years later when I gained an unlikely victory for Wales over him playing squash against Scotland at Edinburgh.

It was his forbear, Dick La Terriere, who wrote to Matt Dawson, who took Fred on as an apprentice without other references and so began one of the greatest trainer/jockey relationships of all time. The child though hated his first year at Newmarket. He was thin, light, overgrown and terrified of the older, stronger boys, who bullied him mercilessly. The one thing the child had was a natural affinity with horses and it was this that carried him through the early months. He had joined a stable which was going from strength to strength and in 1869 Lord Falmouth, one of the greatest owners of his day, joined the stable.

In 1869 his father decided to visit Newmarket to see how Fred was getting on. During the course of the visit they ran into a Mrs Croppy Willan, who was looking for a lightweight jockey for her horse, Maid of Trent, and Fred was duly engaged and won on the filly. This was at Bangor-on-Dee and the race was a Galloway Steeplechase. It was to be another year before Fred had his first flat winner at Chesterfield in September 1870.

In 1871 he was reported with another jockey for misbehaviours at the start and he received two weeks suspension, the only time he ever received a penalty from the Stewards. It has to be said that the rules were very different in those days and a great deal of rough riding went unreported. In 1872 he won one important race, the Cesarewitch, and had twenty-five winners from 136 rides. The following year he was appointed lightweight jockey for the stable and won his first classic, the 2000 Guineas on Atlantic. The next year he became champion jockey for the first time and would dominate the turf until his untimely death. His main rival in the early days was George Fordham, another great jockey, totally unknown by today's racing public. Fordham was a big drinker and alcohol caused him major problems. He hated Epsom, where Archer was always supreme – but the young Archer was also having problems. He had weighed in for his Bangor success at 4 stone 11 pounds but his weight now shot up. He was having to resort to extreme methods of getting it down and this was to spoil his life. His greatest problems concerned his feet and legs which were weak and he had difficulty running, so one of the most popular means of getting rid of weight, long distance running, was denied him. Archer's height had leapt up to 5 foot 8 ½ inches, very tall for any top jockey, and his diet was horrific as a result. According to John Welcome, his breakfast was a tablespoon of hot castor oil and half an orange, for lunch a sardine and a small glass of champagne and the Turkish bath Matt Dawson had installed to sweat the horses now had another regular client.

Another problem was the physical difficulty of actually getting to the races. Although there was by now a good network of train services there was the problem of getting to the right station and where to change. Determined not to miss winners his travelling arrangements must have included tremendous planning.

1875 was another great year for the stable and aged eighteen he was champion jockey again, with 172 wins. 1876 was even better, he won the Derby on Silvio and finished the season with 207 winners (the second had 74).

Whilst money had now started to pour into his pockets, Fred was very generous and particularly so to his parents. His father, who had once told his mother not to bother about schooling, 'the boy will earn money with horses', certainly reaped the benefit. He was set up by his son as proprietor of the Adoversford Hotel. Wealth however did not change Fred, who continued to be as unassuming as ever. His love of hunting meant that he could now, in the winter, go to all the great hunts in the country and during the season he was as likely to be found in Melton Mowbray or Oakham as at home in Gloucestershire. Unfortunately his weight would balloon to eleven stone and the purgatives and Turkish baths became increasingly necessary. His doctor devised a purgative for him that was known as 'Archer's mixture'. A friend who had a tablespoon was unable to get up the next day yet Archer drank it by the glass. Anybody who has had the same problem, and I suffered throughout my twenties trying to play top-class squash, will know that it gets increasingly difficult to get weight off. Aged twenty I could take two or three stone off in a few weeks but as my twenties passed it got more difficult. By twenty-nine, the age of Archer's death, it was nearly impossible.

However nothing stopped Archer's progress; by 1880 he had all the great aristocrats in racing vying for his services. Apart from Lord Falmouth he was riding for and receiving retainers from four Dukes, Hamilton, Portland, Westminster and Beaufort and a leading Earl, Rosebery, no less!

1880 was the year he won the Derby on Bend Or, despite having been previously savaged in the arm by a horse he had once been very severe with and who was determined to get his revenge. He was not really fit enough to take the ride but was determined to do so and got his favourite inside position. However Robert the Devil had such a lead by the straight that no one thought he could be caught and the bookies were laying 10/1 on. Although the gap was closing fast, a hundred yards out Archer, forgetting his useless arm, went for the whip and promptly dropped it. The jockey on Robert the Devil made the classic error of looking round and his horse lost momentum. At the post they were locked together but after a lengthy pause Bend Or got the verdict. Both horse and rider had shown astonishing courage.

The following year, 1881, Dawson, who was childless and had almost adopted Archer, made him a partner. Meanwhile Fred was falling in love with Dawson's brother John's daughter, Helen Rose, described as a small, fair, pretty girl. They became engaged and Archer set about building a large house for his bride – Lord Falmouth helping him with the architect and builder and allowing him to call it Falmouth House.

He finished 1882 as champion again, with 210 winners, and was married on 31st January 1883. All seemed set for another tremendous season but the year was marred by a highly controversial Derby. He won the 2000 Guineas on Gelliard and seemed to have a great chance of following up in the Derby. Lord Falmouth, who owned the horse, was talking of retirement but hoped for a last Derby winner. Unfortunately Fred's brother, Charles, had an enormous bet on Highland Chief, who should have won the race, both being narrowly beaten by St Blaize. The repercussions after the race were immense. Archer was falsely accused by sections of the press of throwing the race to let his brother win his bet which as Highland Chief failed to get the verdict would have been to no avail anyway. The situation was made worse by Lord Falmouth announcing his retirement from racing. Whilst everybody knew he was contemplating retirement the timing was unfortunate. He was later to regret the timing and after dispersing his considerable empire did buy one or two horses which Archer rode for him. Certainly the accusations hurt Archer enormously. That year, his wife was having a very difficult pregnancy and in January 1884 a son was born but died a few hours later. To make matters worse the Duke of Portland gave up his retainer and with it the ride on the best horse around, St Simon. Despite all this 1884 looked like being his best season ever, and with a few days to go he rode a big winner at Liverpool for his great admirer, the old Duchess of Montrose. As he got back to the weighing room he received news that he had a daughter and that both wife and child were both fine. He returned to Falmouth House and everything seemed OK but his sister, who had taken charge, rushed into his room shouting that Helen Rose was desperately ill. Together they found Helen Rose in convulsions and she died without recognising him.

His friends thought he would never recover and one of them, Captain Bowling, told him that for the sake of his child he had to get on with his life. A trip to America was suggested and a lengthy stay there included shooting trips in the wilds and a visit to Canada. He returned just in time for the Lincoln meeting and a season which was to be his greatest ever. His total of 246 winners, including 4 classics, from 667 rides was not beaten for 48 years, when Gordon Richards did so in 1933.

Archer was to ride his fifth Derby winner in 1886 on possibly the best horse he ever rode, Ormonde. This was the only bright sport in the tragedy that was to unfold. At the beginning of November 1886 Archer felt so ill he returned to Falmouth House where two doctors diagnosed Typhoid. His sister, Captain Bowling and two nurses tried to deal with the illness which included the deepest mental depression and although his illness subsided, he put a revolver, which he always had by the side of his bed, to his head and committed suicide.

He was twenty-nine years old and in spite of being one of the greatest jockeys of all time, was a remarkably nice and unassuming man. Only the appalling wasting that he had to endure and his temperament stopped him from living a full life until old age.

Steve Donoghue came from a totally different background from

Fred Archer. Far from the glorious countryside of the Cheviots it was the grimy streets of Warrington that Steve had trodden as a child. He had an extremely tough childhood. Whilst he adored his mother he was terrified of his father, a hard drinking brute who would beat him frequently and severely.

What made him want to be a stable lad is not known but he persuaded a school friend to write to John Porter, the most famous trainer in England, to ask if there were any vacancies – the answer came back that there were none. There things would have rested had Steve not read in his father's racing paper that John Porter was going to Chester races the following week. He skipped school and hitchhiked a series of lifts in the 20 mile journey, discovered where Porter was likely to be and found him saddling his runners. Porter told the young ragamuffin that he must bring his father the next day if he wanted to be a stable lad.

Steve returned to the severest thrashing he had ever received but his mother, having heard the full story, somehow persuaded her husband to accompany the boy to Chester the next day. John Porter accepted the lad, and he managed to get a lift to Kingsclere the following day in a late departing horse box.

Unfortunately the first time he was put up on a thoroughbred he fell off and his horse careered into others causing havoc to the string. He wrote to his mother, who sent him the money for the fare home. He then proceeded to run away from home, taking his younger brother, George, with him. They crossed into Yorkshire and found employment as stable lads with Dobson Peacock at Middleham. Because they had run away they gave their surname as Smith, but this was to have repercussions when the 1901 Census required their father's signature. A hurried departure followed and the two brothers ended up in Newmarket, where they found employment at different stables, Steve for a trainer called Sadler at Freemasons Lodge. Again the problem of a false name arose, when Sadler wanted Steve to sign indentures which required his father's signature. Again he had to move and applied and obtained a job in France for an American trainer, Edward Johnson. In France Donoghue had his first ride in public, in May 1904, but had to wait for his first winner until the next season when he won on a maiden colt called Hanoi at Hyères, named after a little town between Toulon and St Tropez. He followed this with a second winner at Aix les Bains, a major racecourse outside Paris.

Stephen returned to England late in the 1906 season to be told that his brother, riding in Ireland, was not being paid the wages he was due. He went to Ireland to investigate and discovered there was a very good reason for the non-payment – every time his brother got money he would go on a binge taking other stable staff with him. Matthew Dawson persuaded him he should stay and ride in Ireland and in 1907 he started riding numerous winners, finishing the season by winning the Irish Cesarewitch on Mrs Lyons. His weight was 7 stone and he had a natural affinity with horses; he was on the way up. He was also falling in love with Bridgid Behan, the daughter of a trainer he had taken a retainer off. They were married late in 1908 before Stephen started riding regularly in England and after a successful season an operation for a rupture was followed by an attack of Typhoid which put him in hospital and perhaps gave him time for reflection. It was obvious that Stephen would need to move to England to achieve the success his ability demanded and it was fortunate for both parties that he chose Atty Persse at Chattis Hill to take a retainer. Both were masters of their trade and the long partnership that ensued did an enormous amount for both parties. In order to be close to Chattis Steve bought a house, Winton Hill House, half a mile from Stockridge. He employed a chauffeur, gardeners and a cook. A far cry from the grimy back streets of Warrington.

It was 1913 which was to be one of Stephen's great years and a horse called The Tetrarch was to do much to propel him to the very top of the tree. Stephen won three races on him including the Woodcote Stakes at the Derby meeting before riding in the most infamous Derby in history, when Emily Davidson brought down King George's horse, Anmer, she died from her injuries a few days later, but what is fascinating is that today the media frequently bring out the old clips and make out that His Majesty's horse was singled out. That was not the view of either Stephen, who gave evidence, or Anmer's jockey, Herbert Jones, who believed that Davidson was merely trying to cross the course and said she had a look of absolute horror when she was struck into. As I mentioned in Chapter 1 Stephen always maintained that to single out a horse and go for it would be impossible.

A fortnight after the Derby, Steve and The Tetrarch won the Coventry Stakes by 10 lengths and then won again at Sandown's Eclipse meeting but only by a neck at 100/12 on! The horse had in fact got the starting tapes entangled in his mouth and lost nearly a furlong at the start. Three easy victories at Goodwood, Derby and Doncaster (the Champagne) completed a fantastic season for the great horse.

Sadly for Steve the Great War was to interrupt his career and one should remember that he lost almost four years at the peak of his ability. He did try and enlist but was turned down because of the rupture four years earlier.

There is no doubt either that at some point his home life had started to deteriorate and in the winter of 1916 he went to South Africa to ride for Solly Joel, an immensely wealthy mining magnate. On the trip there he met Lady Eleanor Torrington and unlike many ship board meetings, this romance was to be the most enduring of his life. Lady Torrington had married her husband in a haze of the glamorous life style they were both in, but Lord Torrington turned out to be far less wealthy than she expected and at the time of Steve and her meeting he was a prisoner-of-war in Turkey. When Steve returned to England he discovered that his wife, Bridgid, had been unfaithful which gave him the opportunity to intensify his relationship with Lady Torrington, whilst castigating the behaviour of his wife. He sold his Stockbridge house and Bridgid returned to Ireland and in due course a notice appeared in the press: Stephen Donoghue was in the divorce court yesterday and granted a decree Nisi with costs, dissolving the marriage with his wife Bridgid on the grounds of her misconduct with George Walsh, a former jockey and stableman. The suit was uncontested and Stephen was granted custody of the three children. Many of his friends had suggested reconciliation and Bridgid had written begging for forgiveness, a letter Stephen used to considerable effect. It has to be said that in those days all the advantages were with the husband not the wife. Anybody who has read the biographies of Bendor, Duke of Westminster, then the richest man in Britain, would realise how badly treated wives could be and how all the bargaining power was with the husband. There is no doubt either that Stephen's friendship with Lady Torrington made reconciliation with Bridgid impossible and his three children were the big losers, though Lady Torrington did at least find them an excellent nanny and did see, in the early days after the divorce, that they were reasonably looked after.

Once peacetime was restored, racing gradually returned to normal and once again a vastly rich, small coterie of wealthy owners dominated the scene. Stephen had also dominated the jockeys being champion jockey for 10 years in succession from 1914 to 1923. Little was he then to know that a young stable lad who worshipped him and tried to copy his style of riding would take over from him. Amazingly they were also to become firm friends. The up and coming was of course Gordon Richards. In his autobiography he writes warmly of Stephen and gives us an insight into his character. Richards, just starting as a stable lad, said in the second chapter of his book:

> ... a tremendous thrill was the arrival of the stable jockey, the great Steve Donoghue. I was to discover that he was a lovable, carefree

> character, who took everything in his stride. He never got flustered and I never saw him worry about anything. He was immensely popular and he loved his popularity for he was a bit of a showman. The only trouble with Steve is that time meant nothing to him, he would always buy a first-class ticket but would only catch the train as it was moving out, more often ending up in the Guards van. There was no one like Steve on a horse; he had a wonderful gift which was a joy to watch. He would get on a restive horse and the horse would calm down at once. I shall never forget my first meeting with Steve Donoghue at Foxhill, he put us all at our ease straight away. He obviously was happy with us and we were at once happy with him.

A little later in the chapter:

> Steve began to take a real interest in me, I was watching everything Steve did, trying to do the same and gaining confidence. It was extraordinary how the most excitable horse would settle as soon as Steve got on its back. He was part and parcel of the horse, the two became a team. I never took my eyes off him.

Like Fred Archer, Stephen was at his best riding Epsom, a course which defeated many other jockeys – he won the Derby 6 times and the Oaks twice. His three successive Derby winners in 1921, 1922 and 1923 were perhaps the high point of his career. Although Gordon Richards was to take over the mantle of champion jockey and make it his own for over twenty years, Stephen was still a great force in the big races.

By 1926 Steve's fortunes were on the wane. Although immensely popular with both trainers and the public he had upset several leading owners who had retainers with him because he had not always honoured the retainers. He had earned fortunes but as fast as he made money he gave it away and in the late twenties he stunned the racing world by being made bankrupt. This did not stop him riding and, in his last years, a retainer from Sir Victor Sasoon and a wonderful horse, Brown Jack, sustained his enthusiasm. Asked what it was like to ride winners at fifty, he replied that it was a lot better than riding losers.

He turned to training and a succession of top owners made sure he had plenty of horses, but his training career coincided with World War Two and racing was so disrupted that he soon lost heart. He died in 1945 and was buried in Warrington where a statue of him remains today.

Gordon Richards was born in Oakengates, now part of Telford and very close to my father's home, Tickwood Hall, in the hills above

Ironbridge Power Station. His father was a miner who also had pit ponies. Aged fifteen he answered an advertisement from Martin Hartigan for stable staff and departed for Foxhill near Swindon, where Jimmy White, who owned the stables, also employed Steve Donaghue as stable jockey. White offered him a ride at Leicester if he converted a penalty in an inter stable football match and after having to walk his horse, Gay Lord, a total of eight miles from and to the train stations he duly won and then had a double at Lewes three weeks later. His early mentor was Mr Reid Walker, who had a large estate near Shifnal, a few miles from Gordon's birthplace. He would ask Gordon to stay with him for Wolverhampton meetings, where he was a steward. In his book Gordon said Reid Walker had made clear he thought he was destined for great things. When he went to stay he and another jockey had dinner separately but were sent in port before joining the other guests around the billiard table. I never met Mr Reid Walker but his son Gwyn was a great friend of my fathers and used to bring bottles of prime vintage port for father to sample. He did me one great favour when I was 'double banking' behind the line at the Pool, still one of the great drives on the family shoot, Llanarmon. Gwyn had a terrible hangover and rushed to be ill behind a hedge, shouting at me to take his place. To my amazement, firing a lot more cartridges than usual, I began to hit a lot of birds and my shooting, which had been in the doldrums, took off from that day.

At the dinners at Tickwood, Gwyn would talk about Gordon Richards and particularly about the family billiard table where a lot of excitement took place. I only wish I had taken more notice but I do remember the grown-ups talking about another subject, their favourite shipping lines, as air travel had only just started in the late forties early fifties. I remember Gwyn saying to father, 'Jimmy, I always take Italian boats – there is none of this nonsense of women and children first on them.' I thought of Gwyn when I read about the Italian captain on the *Concordia*; some things never change! Mr Reid Walker senior was a steward at Wolverhampton where I was to begin my stewarding career some forty years later. He was to teach Gordon one sharp lesson, when he fined him twenty-five pounds (a lot of money in those days) for being five minutes late for the first race.

However 1926 was not to be his year as he contracted tuberculosis and spent months in a Norfolk sanatorium. A fellow patient was Bill Rowell, who was to become a mentor to Richards, teaching him how to cope with the riches that were coming his way.

From 1927 onwards Gordon was to dominate the jockeys championship in the same way that A.P. McCoy has done in National

Hunt racing in recent years. When in 1933 he beat Fred Archer's record he was unstinting in his praise of Archer. Archer, he said, had only one advantage, he did not have to draw for places – he could generally take up the position he wanted. In every other way he had the advantage over Archer. Archer was 5ft 10″, Gordon Richards 4ft 11 ½″, Archer could never get below 8st 8lbs, Richards could ride below 8st. Archer had to waste incessantly, Richards never had to. The travelling Archer had to do was vastly greater than Richards. In Gordon Richards opinion Archer's feat of riding 246 winners in a season is the greatest feat by a jockey of all time.

The war years were to curtail Richards's tally of winners, though he rode some great horses. He had tried hard to enlist but had failed his medical because of his chest problems in the twenties. The Derby was transferred to Newmarket, the St Leger to Manchester or Thirsk. In a way it was sad that Sun Chariot and Big Game, both owned by His Majesty George VI, ran in wartime classics. They were both good enough to win most peacetime ones and, as Gordon said afterwards, Sun Chariot was such a brilliant filly she would have won most Derbys.

Gordon was also helped by his two main retainers, Fred Darling, the master of Beckhampton, and the Aga Khan, just about the richest owner in the world. He managed his retainers far better than Steve Donaghue who was always in trouble for breaking his agreements to ride fancied horses in big races. Fred Darling and Gordon had a wonderful relationship, probably the best ever between a great trainer and a great jockey. Gordon Richards is also the only flat jockey in this chapter who resided mainly outside Newmarket. He was there briefly in his early days but whilst he loved the course he disliked the gallops and much preferred the serenity of Berkshire.

After the war racing gradually got back to normal, Richards was particularly pleased that Newmarket's old course – in his opinion, the best in the world – was reopened. Darling's three-year-olds were not good and Richards was aided by his Aga Khan retainer where he rode Tehran against Ocean Swell, two great horses. He managed to finish champion jockey in 1945 but with a total of just over 100.

The end of the war enabled Richards to get back to the one place in Europe he really loved, St. Moritz. Whilst his one sport, curling, can't have tackled his stamina too much he was to rely on the wonderful air there more and more as he got older. He must have drunk a lot less than we all did in the three years I went to St. Moritz; I always came away feeling I needed a holiday.

In fact 1944 had been a bad year for Richards as he suffered a near nervous breakdown and an ulcer and the stress he was enduring continued on after the war ended. He was extremely lucky to have a totally loyal and sensible wife and Margery must have gone through hell coping with him in these difficult times. She eventually persuaded him to see his doctor in London, Doctor Slesinger, and he recounts how just before Goodwood the doctor persuaded him to go to Switzerland, drink some champagne and then go back to normal race riding.

This brought a flood of memories back for me. I can only say that Doctor Slesinger would have been well aware of the benefits of champagne. His house near Lingfield was awash with it whenever I have stayed there.

1947 was an eventful year for Gordon – he broke his own record riding 269 winners – but not all went right for him. Another wonderful horse, Tudor Minstrel, was his to ride and he won the 2000 Guineas by 8 lengths. Expected to win the Derby easily, he failed to act at Epsom and Richards suddenly found himself heavily criticised – something he definitely was not used to. In fact the Derby was the one race that eluded him until late in his career.

Having got over all his mental problems 1953 and 1954 were to be decent years. However age was beginning to catch up with him and Dr. Slesinger was on hand to persuade him to take three weeks off early in the 1953 season and have massage and treatment and it was the following year that two tremendous events took place. The first was a letter from the Prime Minister telling him that the Queen was to award him a Knighthood. He was to be very deservedly the first and so far only jockey to receive that honour and not unnaturally he was over the moon. He met the Prime Minister, Winston Churchill, at Lingfield Park races a few days later, who asked him if he had received his letter. 'I did sir,' Richards replied, 'and I answered it last night!' Richards was to meet the Queen just before the Derby and she stopped him and wished him luck.

His mount, Pinza, was a magnificent horse and although Richards had been trying to win the Derby for years he would never have a better chance. He had taken unusual trouble in riding work on Pinza at Newmarket, which entailed much more travelling than normal, but when the race came he could not have been on an easier winner, always well placed and the crowd calling him a long way from the post. Ironically Her Majesty, who had recently knighted him, had the second, Aureole, a very good horse who in another year could have been a worthy winner. Richards rated Pinza as one of the best horses he had ever seen. His owner, Sir Victor Sasoon, had put an immense amount of money into racing and he too more than deserved a Derby winner. Sadly after he had won the King George, Pinza broke down.

Course watering systems were unheard of and gallops could be bone hard and Pinza was a big horse. He might have fared even better in current conditions.

Gordon Richards retired in 1954 following an injury to his pelvis. His magnificent career had brought him 4870 wins and unlike his two great predecessors in this chapter, there was very little controversy attached to him at any point. He was to live for another 34 years, training with reasonable success and then acting as racing manager to Lady Beaverbrook and Lord Weinstock. His record of being 26 times champion jockey may never be beaten and he was a great credit to his profession.

Lester Piggott could not have been more different from Gordon Richards. Born three years after me in 1935, he was very tall at 5ft 8" for a flat jockey, possibly fractionally smaller than Fred Archer. Like Fred Archer he needed to diet continuously to keep himself to a reasonable riding weight of just over eight stone but unlike Fred Archer, he adopted Spartan habits at an early age. This I can vouch for myself, having seen him in the winter – he rarely allowed himself any excesses at any time of the year.

He came from a family steeped in racing; indeed he is the only one of the five flat jockeys I have written about who can boast this claim. Although Lester's grandfather, Ernie, owned a stable at Letcombe Regis and his father, Keith, at South Bank, Lambourn, where Lester was brought up, the family roots go back to Cheshire. For a long time the Piggotts had a farm there and ran the Crown Inn at Nantwich at the end of the eighteen hundreds. Both Ernie and Keith were successful National Hunt jockeys, Ernie rode the winner of the Grand National in 1912, 1918 and 1919 and Keith won the Champion Hurdle as a jockey in 1939 and trained Ayala, which I had the good fortune to back at 100/1, for hairdresser 'Mr Teasy Weasy'. On his mother's side Lester was a first cousin to Bill and Fred Rickaby. Bill Rickaby was retained by my family for many years and rode my wonderful stayer, Precipice Wood, as a two-year-old and had he stayed on instead of retiring would undoubtedly have helped enormously to shape his three-year-old career. He died tragically in a road accident in Hong Kong.

Lester was, like Fred Archer, a precocious child, who was to start riding his father's horses at ten years old and had his first winner at Haydock Park on a horse called The Chase at the age of twelve.

His determination and precociousness at such an early age gained him great support from the average racegoer but the opposite from the Jockey Club and racecourse Stewards, who regarded his riding with suspicion and gave it plenty of attention. His speech impediment led to many imitations of his voice and also helped to shape his character. The word taciturn would not have been out of place. His brush with authority came early in his career when he received a six month suspension and was ordered to spend it away from his father's stable. Rightly or wrongly, the Jockey Club were convinced Keith Piggott was not a good influence on his son. His winning the Derby at the age of eighteen on Never Say Die established him still further as the darling of the public. His racing career very much compares with Gordon Richards, though the two characters could not have been more different.

Lester Piggott's character is very difficult for an outsider like myself to sum up because he is frankly, quite unlike anybody else I have ever come across. His attitude to money is the stuff legends are made of. I first came across it on holiday in the Bahamas at the end of the fifties, when my mother, a friend of Lady Barnsie Sassoon, engineered my appearance at the Sassoon swimming pool and a very interesting trip on a Saturday to Hialeah Racecourse. Very naïve in those days I couldn't understand Lester's miserliness, or whatever other words you want to call it. His attitude was simply, I have made a lot of money through my own ability and nobody is going to touch it. I was also to witness, at first hand, his determination to stick to his Spartan diet. The only time in his riding career I have seen him remotely let his hair down was at the party Robert Sangster gave in Annabel's private room, after The Minstrel's victory, where he did make some attempt to eat and drink something and join in the general conviviality (to put it very mildly!).

As I have written elsewhere, Lester only rode for me once, on Cormorant Wood in the Oaks. I am still quite sure he could have been fourth but once he saw he was not going to win the race, he lost interest and with it eight thousand pounds (a lot of money in the early eighties) and good black type for a very valuable mare. What was even more disastrous for me was that he made no attempt to tell us the real reason she didn't win the Oaks, i.e. she didn't stay the mile and a half. This was to cost me vastly more money than the eight thousand and was, I fear, typical of Lester, who had many good points but unselfishness was not one of them.

When I was privileged to sit in on a major discussion between Vincent O'Brien and Robert Sangster at Ballydoyle (I had gone over with Robert) I can still remember Vincent saying to Robert, 'We have the best jockey in the world but the one thing I do not want is for him to continue to come over and ride work. He takes no interest in a word I tell him, all he wants to do is find out which really are the best horses and I want to keep that for you and I, Robert, not for the stable jockey.' In fairness to Lester I would have to say that his lifestyle was very different to both Robert and Vincent's, they were big drinkers (as indeed I was) and wanted to get some fun out of their many great triumphs. They would have liked their jockey to join in but that was not Lester's style at all and not even for his principal owner and trainer was he going to change it.

His obsessive attitude to money was of course going to cost him his liberty when he failed to stop the Inland Revenue bringing a case against him for tax fraud. I well remember that for a good period before the case, the racing gossip was full of Lester's refusal to give in to the Inland Revenue and surely had he taken any sensible advice, his jail sentence could have been avoided. I have no idea whether the story going the rounds was true or not, that when he finally paid them a cheque, it was with a bank that the Inland Revenue had no idea that Lester had an account with. 'I love it.'

In fact, I, like most of the racing world, was very saddened by the jail sentence and still more so with the withdrawal of his OBE, where I, like many others, would have liked to have seen the rules bent for once. By a coincidence I did have an old school friend who twice went to see Lester in jail. According to him the first time he went Lester was miserable and told him that his cellmate was in for GBH. I suspect my friend might have used some influence (he was a registered prison visitor) because the second time he went his cellmate turned out to be someone who had owned horses and Lester was much more cheerful.

Lester had been training quite successfully prior to the jail sentence but made little attempt to resume when he came back to a handful of horses in the stable. His second time as a jockey came when he made a comeback aged 54. Again the stuff legends are made of. Within ten days of his return he rode the winner of the Breeders Cup mile on Royal Academy, an incredible feat. I have written in the chapter on Stewarding about the Vernon Sprint Cup, when he came third to a horse of Robert Sangster's. He objected to the first two, although he had no chance of improving his placing; he had sensed that first and second had come close together and wanted to stir things up, which he certainly did. He was always wanting something to happen and as his life was totally dedicated to riding winners, there was little time for anything else.

His riding career was amazing – thirty classic winners which included nine Derbys. He was flat racing champion jockey eleven times and that included a gap of ten years, so he did not ride continuously like Sir Gordon.

He could be very hard on his horses. His ride on Roberto in the Derby is etched in my memory and I wonder what suspension he would have got under current whip rules. Yet very few jockeys, past or present, would have got Roberto home that day.

Lester's whole life was racing and he was always incredibly knowledgeable, knowing the history of all the top horses overseas as well. He was supreme at Epsom and once told me he liked riding at Chester because he could ride the course better than most of the others. Modesty was certainly not part of his make up!

The one time I saw him utterly relaxed and thoroughly enjoying himself was in Cape Town, where he was on holiday with his then girlfriend and his small son. Never a person to be the least interested in convention, he was utterly at ease with the child and perhaps in old age he was at last able to relax and lead a more normal life.

When his relationship with Robert Sangster and Vincent O'Brien came to an end in 1980 he was appointed stable jockey to Henry Cecil but he was to fall out with Henry's principal owner, Daniel Wildenstein, and in 1984 Cecil and Piggott split up and Steve Cauthen left Barry and Robert to take Lester's place at Henry Cecil's stables, Warren Place. He was to succeed undoubtedly one of the greatest ever flat jockeys.

Again **Steve Cauthen** could not have been a more different character to Lester. Robert Sangster, who was having quite a number of horses with Barry Hills, made him an offer to come to England as first jockey for Barry. Although only 18 years old, Steve had had great success in America, where he had been champion jockey and won their triple crown on Affirmed. Steve and I actually became good friends very quickly and having come from a country background in Kentucky, with reasonably well off parents who had brought him up sensibly, he took to English life like a duck to water. He had his first winner at Salisbury and won the 2000 Guineas on Tap On Wood, the start of a great period for him. He was soon staying with Angela and I during our brief period at Sweetenham and having heard about the family shoot at Llanarmon, he asked for an invitation and I got him into the second main shoot in late November. We all stayed at the Hand Hotel, then owned by my father, and gathered round the bar. He was asked by another guest if he had done a lot of pheasant shooting. 'Never shot one in my life, sir.' He replied. Put on the outside of the line he shot 7 at the first stand and by the middle of the second day he was shooting as well as half the line.

He entered into every aspect of English life and that included the heavy partying that Robert and I were liable to get into. Although he only really liked one drink, champagne, he developed a real thirst for it. Far more serious was the habit he had got into, common to many American jockeys, of vomiting food to keep his weight down. In fact in some American jockeys rooms there were bowls for that purpose.

It was Angela, who had been anorexic herself when young, who realised what Steve was doing, although both Barry and I were oblivious to the problem. I had arranged a gourmet dinner party for him of caviar followed by grouse and then ice cream. He had 2 large portions of caviar, two grouse (one was extra in case one was not a tender young grouse) and three portions of ice cream, going to the Cloakroom at regular intervals. After dinner he asked if he could watch the late night film and Angela and I were nearly asleep when there was a crash downstairs. That will be Steve at the fridge, said Angela, who found him happily munching away with a bag of apples in one hand and biscuits in the other. None of this seemed to affect his riding and he went from strength to strength, leaving Barry for Henry Cecil and gaining the most prized contract of all, a retainer from Sheik Mohammed.

He had two beautiful girlfriends, the first being Caroline Herbert, the daughter of Lord Porchester (later the Earl of Carnarvon). She and Steve came to Llanarmon to stay with us for a two-day shoot and we all had great fun. On the Monday she rang me, sounding very subdued, to say that her father had taken a very dim view of how she had spent the weekend and he virtually ended the romance, which Steve took extremely badly. Her father did not stop her marrying John Warren, now the Queen's racing manager and happily that marriage has been long and happy.

His next and final girlfriend before Amy, who became his wife, arrived from America, was Annabel Croft, then becoming England's top woman tennis player. Again we all had a lot of fun together and I have two regrets, one that Angela and I didn't go to her twenty-first party and two that I didn't produce her as my secret weapon in a regular four I had with Panton Corbett and another friend at Queen's Club.

Steve produced two rides for me which are unforgettable: The Champion Stakes, where he came from last to first in the last two furlongs in a gale I can only repeat the words of Richard Berlein in the press the next day, 'Steve Cauthen rode a miraculous race, of all his brilliant performances in the second half of the season, none has equalled this stroke of genius.' *Racehorses of 1983* wrote 'the winner, Cormorant Wood, produced a performance that had to be seen to be believed. With superb assistance from Cauthen, she came from last to first in the final three furlongs, sweeping past tightly packed contestants being buffeted by a gale force wind, she swept up the hill on the bridle and at the very last found enough room between Tolemeo and the only other filly in the race, Flame of Tara, to lift the prize.

Her performance the following year in the Benson and Hedges International (now the Juddmonte) whilst not as spectacular was equally mind blowing. Saddlers Wells started a strong favourite but in a summer of bone hard ground, which did not suit us, York had managed to produce decent going. We had all walked the course carefully as we had vowed not to run her again on hard ground, which both Royal Ascot and Sandown (the Eclipse) had. This was the first time since the Champion Stakes she had really good ground and she revelled in it. Steve saw she was going so well coming into the straight that he went back two places to get a good run to the finish. We never had a moment's worry and she won easily, beating Tolomeo by much further than in the Champion Stakes. The thrill of having one of the greatest world class jockeys on board the best flat racehorse I will ever own, is something beyond description.

As I say Steve's career went from strength to strength but he ended the 1993 season only sixth in the flat jockeys list, having lost his retainer from Sheikh Mohammed and retired, to live happily with Amy in Kentucky and lead a normal family life with his children. I believe he has done some commentating and breeding of racehorses. Thanks for everything Steve!

A.P. McCoy became champion National Hunt jockey in 1996 having been conditional champion jockey in the previous year. From then on until his retirement this year, 2015, he dominated the National Hunt scene in the same way Gordon Richards had dominated the flat jockeys. There have, in the past thirty years, been many good National Hunt jockeys, names like Dunwoody, Francombe, Scudamore, Williamson and many others stand out, but McCoy surpasses all of them. Born May 1974 in Moneyglass, Northern Ireland, he was to ride four thousand three hundred and forty-eight winners over jumps and nine on the flat before choosing his own retirement date at Sandown on April 25th 2015.

A.P. is universally liked and has lived a happy family life and despite his numerous achievements is far from flamboyant, although his number plate incorporating AP 4000, signals his presence on any racecourse. Although I have met him racing many times I cannot claim to know him well. The two stories I regularly tell about him are my encounter with him at Uttoxeter some years ago, already told elsewhere in this book, when Paul Webber and I had a near certainty in a maiden hurdle but he persuaded us that the ground was too firm to run a good horse, which mine was, and then won the race himself after several withdrawals including mine. The day was a memorable one for Paul and I as Stanley Clarke, whose instructions to his Clerk of the Courses was always put the word 'Good' in the your going report, said to both of us, 'You are like a lot of sheep.' He did later apologise to Paul for his remark.

My other memorable encounter was on the golf course, when I headed an Aintree team to have a fun day at Sunningdale with National Hunt jockeys. Golf is the main relaxation of many National Hunt jockeys who are fiercely competitive and almost invariably have handicaps which do not totally tally with their expertise. I was a long time member of Sunningdale, a great course which has strict rules, one of which totally bans mobile phones on the course. To my horror A.P. and the other two jockeys all produced mobile phones on the first two holes. I attempted to say please don't use them or we will all be very unpopular but I was talking to deaf ears. A.P. was by far the worst of the three, his phone never stopped ringing and he insisted on answering it. The result was that the game took forty-five minutes longer than it should have done and as I moved through the members bar to the members changing room an elderly member said to me, 'I thought I saw the champion jockey out on the course.' I replied that he was correct and he then said, 'I hope they remembered our rule about mobile phones.' With a straight face I replied, 'Of course they did.'

How did A.P. become so dominant? A former colleague who knows him well said that although he was too tall to become a flat jockey he had relatively short legs which enabled him to ride like a flat jockey and that as a result he had a low centre of gravity. He also had an excellent agent, Dave Roberts, who McCoy rarely questioned and the partnership between the two gave McCoy the minimum of worry over planning his rides. He was also fortunate in his main retainers, joining Martin Pipe in 1997 after a spell with Toby Balding as a conditional jockey. That followed an apprenticeship with Jim Bolger where he rode his first winner in 1992, aged seventeen, in a flat race at Thurles. His first serious fall was to be riding work, when he fell and broke his leg on the gallops.

His retainer with J.P. McManus later in life was the most prized and remunerative in National Hunt racing and he joined forces with one of the nicest owners in racing whose main trainer in England, Jonjo O'Neill, was a highly competent jockey himself.

I have been fortunate to get to know many leading jockeys under both rules. Jimmy Lindley, who rode my Ascot Gold Cup winner, came to Llanarmon that winter and was underneath one of the highest birds Precipice Wood has ever produced. He got down on his knees and put his hands up to the heavens to the immense amusement of the other guns. Joe Mercer also came regularly to Llanarmon and his company has always been most enjoyable. Whilst he shot very well at lower bird shoots in the south, I would have to say really high birds were not his speciality. Willie Carson only rode once for me and unfortunately the filly he was on got a bad bump coming out of the stalls. Hunting was Willie's sport and twice he came to our Boxing Day meets, where I always tried to get him to drink a second glass of the port I provided. His wife Elaine, whose parents lived a few miles from us, has always been a good friend of Angela's.

Chapter 8

Racecourses

Although racecourses date back to the beginning of the sixteenth century, it was not until the 1870s that they were ordered to become enclosed with the proper railings to mark their boundaries. Up to this point every town or village of consequence had its own racecourse but the authorities' requirements knocked out many of the smaller ones. By 1900 the fixture list was taking shape and bore a resemblance to the present day version. Although I have been unable to find a record of courses that closed before 1900, there is a definite record since that date, when almost a hundred have sadly bitten the dust. The two World Wars accounted for many of these as with no racing for a significant period, some did not reopen when hostilities ceased.

A typical small courses closure was Oswestry and Llanymynerch, enthusiastically supported by my grandfather between the wars and until I was burgled, a couple of years ago, I was the proud possessor of four large silver cups he had won there. There have been two excellent books published recently dating the history of racing at Oswestry and its surrounds from 1719 onwards. Its final fixture, on May 4th 1940, drew a crowd of 5146 paying racegoers. There are many current National Hunt courses who would have been delighted with that attendance.

Whilst many of the small National Hunt tracks were subsidised by local aristocrats and were allied to hunts, flat courses generally existed on their own merits. Hull racecourse was a typical example. Racing started there in 1760 and flourished until 1796, when George Herring, who had won the previous year's St Leger, was killed there. No further racing took place until 1888, when a completely new course, with large stands, saw an enthusiastic crowd totalling over 34,000 over two days. Sadly the enthusiasm was not to last, though racing continued to 1909. Various attempts were made to restart it, the last being in 1947, but Hull City Council refused to sanction a resumption.

Although the period 1942 to the present day accounted for less closures, some of these were very major courses included Birmingham,

Manchester, Hurst Park and Lincoln.

Both Birmingham and Manchester were fine tracks but their proximity to the city centre was to be their undoing. Racing started at Birmingham in 1895 with meetings on both a flat and National Hunt course, but came to an end in 1965 when Birmingham Corporation bought the track for housing. Now the M6 runs over the remains of a once great course.

Unlike Birmingham, Manchester might have been saved if its shareholders had not been so eager to cash in on their holdings. Racing started in 1647 and by the twentieth century Manchester was a major racecourse with group races on both its tracks. The November handicap will be remembered by veterans like myself. Sold to a developer for housing in 1963, the planning permissions the developer was after were refused and the course finished up as playing fields and halls of residence for Salford College of Technology.

Hurst Park was a very popular course on the edge of the Thames, within a mile of Kempton Park on the other side of the river. Racing started with a jumps meeting in 1890 and a flat meeting a year later. It made front page news in 1913, when Emily Davison's death in the Derby four days earlier had set feelings at boiling point and the main stand was set alight and partially burnt down. The course flourished between the wars, with the best National Hunt horse of the era, Golden Miller, winning one race from three appearances. The flat meetings drew large crowds and after World War II it continued to be popular but was also attracting attention from developers and like Manchester, its owner could see larger profits from a sale rather than from racing. In 1961, following a public enquiry, the course was purchased by the Wates family for £905,000 and racing finished the following year. The Wates family have been great supporters of racing subsequently.

Lincoln, with its big mile handicap, run on the first day of the flat season, was steeped in history. King James I attended racing there in April 1617, though the first mention of horse racing dates back to 1597. By 1680 racing had become an annual event but it was not until 1826 that the first grandstand was built. The best horse to run on the Carholme, as Lincoln's heath was called, was Sceptre, a filly who won both Guineas, the Oaks and the St Leger. In 1902 she started off the season in the Lincolnshire Handicap and under a large weight was beaten a head by a four-year-old.

After the Second World War the crowds started to dwindle; only the Lincolnshire handicap day was attracting a decent crowd. Its owners, Lincolnshire Corporation, had not helped with their fierce opposition to foxhunting, which put off many rural supporters. In April 1963 the Levy Board announced it was one of twelve courses they were not going to support, Lanark and Lewes being two others. The last meeting took place in 1964, Bruce Hobbs training the last winner.

The demise of Lewes means that few people now see the tombstone in a corner of the paddock which marked the grave of Shaun Spadah, winner of the Grand National in 1921 and second two years later. It was his owner, Sir Malcolm McAlpine, whose tales of the race sparked my initial interest in racing.

The Levy Board's decision to withdraw support from twelve courses led to the last substantial group to close down and four new groupings emerged, which form the courses in existence today. They are Jockey Club Racecourses, large independents, smaller independents and ARC, an amalgamation of Arena Leisure and Northern Racing. All racecourses belong to a trade body, the Racecourse Association, but the groupings have little in common and reaching agreements between them can be difficult.

Jockey Club racecourses are a mixture of large and small flat and National Hunt courses and include Epsom, Newmarket, Sandown, Kempton, Haydock, Cheltenham and Aintree. Because of the heavy burden of the Pattern, their profits come almost entirely from the two large National Hunt courses, Cheltenham and Aintree, Cheltenham being by some way the most profitable course in the country. It is a sobering thought that had these two courses not been taken over by the Jockey Club, racing today might look very different.

The large independents are Ascot, York, Goodwood, Chester, Newbury and Ayr. The first four should all be very profitable but the last two struggle in this respect.

The smaller independents are a mixture of flat and National Hunt courses, many of which are the backbone of racing and have mixed fortunes, though the injection of media rights has kept their financial viability intact, though many would prosper in their own right.

ARC has one jewel in the crown, Doncaster, and a number of all weather courses. It is the most unpredictable of the four groupings, sometimes coming up with policies which upset the rest of the industry. Unfortunately before the merger Arena Leisure lost Raymond Mould as chairman, a man who really understood the economics of racing. They have since closed down Folkestone and Hereford and reneged on prize money intentions. They do seem to be out of tune with the other racecourse groupings.

I have graded the individual courses to a formula of my own, which is based on their value to racing as a whole and takes into account current profitability, historic importance, attendance, Pattern involvement etc.

and which is sure to be disputed by many readers who will think I am being unfair to their favourite course and may also think my beloved Chester is too high up.

I have no problem with number one, **Ascot**, owned by the crown and with a reigning monarch who take a great interest in the course. It is appropriate that another female reigning monarch, Queen Anne, was responsible for the laying out of the course in 1711 but it was a much less popular monarch who instigated the Royal Procession, namely George IV, though he was Prince of Wales at the time, 1820.

Ascot has two great courses, flat and National Hunt. The flat course has two different mile races, one the straight mile, run on a very wide track which is slightly uphill for most of the way. Because of the width, large fields often break up into different groups and how the race is run may depend on the lead horses in each group. The alternative mile, known as the old mile, starts at Swinley Bottom and is a straight, uphill run of five furlongs before the three furlong home straight. The course also has the longest flat race in the calendar, the Queen Alexandra Stakes, over two miles six furlongs, the last race of the Royal meeting. Widely criticised by purists, I always found it a fascinating, getting out race and I had one memorable occasion when Jeremy Tree had the favourite. Knowing he hated anybody approaching him for a tip, I bravely went up to him just before the race and said, 'Jeremy I know you hate anyone asking your opinion but I am desperate enough to want to know whether you fancy your horse?' With a look of absolute fury and a long pause he replied, 'Bobby if you have to know, yes I do.' The horse won easily.

If the two courses largely draw praise from those who go racing, the same cannot be said of the stand, probably the most controversial ever to be built. I will never forget the Royal meeting at which it was unveiled as I was as fooled as anybody, having a very pleasant lunch with the Tote board, four floors up. Close by were all the racing scribes, who the Ascot authority had had the good sense to ply with free food and drink. It was only the following day when I sought out my bookmaker, that I realised what a total shambles was taking place down below. You literally could not see the racing at all from the ground floor and the rectification of this alone was to cost over twenty million. By the end of the meeting, a barrage of criticism hit the media and the numbers going to the meeting in the following year took a real caning, though the main reason for building the stand was to accommodate the growing numbers. From my personal point of view I was just as saddened to lose the old paddock and pre-parade ring. The thrill of having a runner at Royal Ascot and walking from the old pre-parade ring to the old paddock could only be understood by those who experienced it.

The one lesson to be learnt is to be very careful not to let the architects control everything. In my construction days we dreaded the architect controlling the building work. Whilst we appreciated the design expertise, we also felt others oversaw the building work more effectively and in this case apparently the height of the viewing steps had not taken into account people would be wearing top hats.

As I was keeping an eye on the new stand at Aintree, on behalf of the board, I was terrified we had made the same mistakes as Ascot and a meeting was convened at Aintree for the following Monday and I spent three or four semi sleepless nights before discovering on the Monday that our architect had got his sight lines right.

Ascot has been a very lucky course for me. I have won four races at the Royal meeting, the Ascot Gold Cup itself, at the tender age of thirty-nine, the King George V handicap, a year earlier with the same horse, Precipice Wood and the Windsor Castle with Rollahead. I should have won the Ascot Stakes with Coed Cochion but his normally very good jockey, Paul Cook, was 'kidded' by Lester Piggott, half way through the race, that they were going too fast and let our pacemaker win at sixty-six to one. To make matters worse I had tried to buy a share in the pacemaker but the Omani owner refused my offer! Finally I won the Queen Alexandra with Coed Cochion.

Ascot has ten Group One races, the latest addition being the Champion Stakes from Newmarket. Whilst Newmarket has too much of the Pattern, the change of venue brought much comment as the two tracks could not be more different and the ground at Newmarket is far more likely to be better in October. However, the crowd on Champions Day at Ascot will be over twice, perhaps three times that of Newmarket.

The National Hunt course is overshadowed by Cheltenham and Aintree but has some valuable meetings and Grade One races, including the Long Walk Hurdle, the Clarence House Chase and the Ascot Chase.

Ascot's chief executive was Charles Barnett, who did a tremendous job at Aintree, under some difficult circumstances. He has been succeeded by Guy Henderson.

Cheltenham is the greatest National Hunt course in the world. Its four-day festival meeting in March, outdoes any other jumps meeting – only Grand National day at Aintree has the crowds and excitement that the Cheltenham festival engenders. Although the Cheltenham Gold Cup is regarded as the ultimate test of a chaser, the Grand National has a larger television audience worldwide.

Cheltenham has three courses: the old course, the new course and the cross country steeplechase course. The Gold Cup is run on the new course and is regarded as the supreme test of a chaser's stamina, jumping ability and versatility under intense pressure. There is a steep downhill run into the home turn and then an uphill finish, which has varied in length over the years.

The Cross Country course is a relatively new addition and whilst popular with a section of the Irish National Hunt fraternity it has not found favour with many onlookers. Punters are bemused at the variations of the track and the majority of bookmakers would prefer it had not been built.

The Festival meeting caters for all types of National Hunt horses over various distances but perhaps the four most important races are: the Gold Cup for staying chasers over three miles two furlongs and one hundred and ten yards. The Queen Mother Champion Chase for speedier, shorter distance chasers, over two miles. The Champion Hurdle, over two miles one hundred and ten yards and the World Hurdle over three miles.

The course has been extremely well managed in recent years. Only marginally profitable when Sam Vestey and Edward Gillespie arrived on the scene in the nineteen seventies, both then being in their twenties when they became chairman and managing director, they have headed a staff who have made the racecourse the most profitable in the country. The Jockey Club is currently funding their most ambitious project to date, with a new main stand and other work which hopefully should help the overcrowding of the most popular Festival meeting in the National Hunt calendar. The current chairman is an accomplished businessman and the chief executive was formerly with ARC, where he worked under a chief executive and is regarded as a very safe pair of hands.

York is the second oldest course in the country, racing having started there in the first half of the sixteenth century, although it was not until 1731 that, after several venues had been tried, racing settled on the Knavesmire, where it has thrived ever since. It is remarkable that the two oldest centres of racing in the country, Chester and York, still vie with each other for the second largest daily attendance (Ascot being the first).

York is a truly great racecourse and a very fair track, a left-handed course on flat ground, which was enlarged in 2005 to hold the Royal meeting and run the Ascot Gold Cup over two-and-a-half miles. Its latest stand is the most successful and best designed of recent stands and the racecourse is extremely popular. It is owned by a trust which allows its directors to offer subsidised food and drink and plough money back into racing. It has two Festival meetings a year, one in May and the other in August, the Ebor meeting in August being the better attended of the two. It has three Group One races and seven Group Two and the Ebor Handicap is the richest handicap in Europe.

The International Stakes, now sponsored by Juddmonte, leads the Group One and I won it with Cormorant Wood in 1984, when the favourite, Sadler's Wells, was fourth. Sadly it was to be Cormorant Wood's last race as she sustained an injury which came to light following the race, her finest!

I once took some champagne lovers from Cheshire, who could not believe the prices of top champagne and stayed there at the Ebor meeting until they were politely told it was time to leave. Fortunately I had made an earlier exit. The course has a long serving, popular, chief executive and the chairmanship changes regularly. It is a very well run course.

Aintree is the home of the Grand National, the most watched race in the world, its television audience being enormous. The National was first run in 1836 on land leased from Lord Sefton, his lordship being the starter for the race. Three years later, a race known as the Grand Liverpool Steeplechase was run closer to the conditions of the present day and is considered by many to be the first proper running.

Many of racing's most exciting characters of the nineteenth century featured in Aintree's early runnings of the race, particularly Captain Becher, who lent his name to the famous fence. When Peter Daresbury and I went to view its reconstruction, some twenty years ago, Peter turned to me and said, 'I hope the Captain doesn't get out of his grave and clobber us for what we have done to his fence.' What he would say now the fence has been further downgraded for the safety brigade, one shudders to think.

My Uncle Tom (Sir Malcolm McAlpine) won the race in 1921 with Shaun Spadah, the only horse to finish, though two were remounted to take second and third. He came second two years later.

Although Golden Miller was the greatest chaser between the World Wars and won the Cheltenham Gold Cup five times, he only won the Grand National once. The most remarkable horse after the war was Red Rum, who won three times with ever increasing weights. If there was an Aintree specialist, it was him.

The race now bears no resemblance to the National of old, the cores of the fences have been altered to make them far less stiff and horses jump them with some ease. The dangers are the speed they can now go at the fences, which also results in tiredness in a long and punishing race. The great advantage of the 'new' fences is that top-class horses now take part and the National has become a very good long distance chase.

The Aintree festival follows Cheltenham with immense prize money and being a completely different course can be ideal for some Cheltenham losers. It has two courses, the National course, which is two circuits of the course over four miles, three and a half furlongs. Thirty fences are jumped, the Chair and the Water Jump are only jumped on the first circuit. The second course is very sharp and has standard fences, although they used to be quite stiff.

Aintree is the Jockey Club's second most profitable course. If all the television rights for the meeting were credited to it, Aintree would be closer to Cheltenham in profitability. Its problems are the other meetings which generate nothing like the support the National meeting has from the public.

Apart from the National it has some other top-class races at its April festival meeting over the Mildmay fences and hurdles. It is truly remarkable that jumping's second great course was nearly lost to the developers twice and much credit must go to three men who were at the forefront of the 'Save Aintree' group, Johnny Henderson and Tommy Wallis, both leading lights in the Jockey Club, and Ivan Straker, who persuaded his company, Seagrams, to sponsor the course for many years. Ivan actually had a heart attack after watching his horse come second in the National.

The course has lost its long-serving chairman, Peter Daresbury, who did a great deal for it, but Rose Paterson, who has taken his place is very able and as the wife of a former cabinet minister, who served for a time as Minister for Northern Ireland, is used to having to deal with people in high office.

Newmarket has been the traditional centre of racing since the reign of James I, who started royal patronage in 1605, though the racing of horses very much took second place to shooting partridges – in fact the king spent so much time there that a delegation was sent from Westminster to ask him to come back and attend to affairs of state. When his son, Charles I, a much better horseman, succeeded him, he was already tainted with his father's actions and was quickly accused of behaving in a similar fashion. Historians differ as to how much time Charles I spent at Newmarket. Two authors of a book on Newmarket, Richard Onslow and Frank Siltzer, have Charles I's first spell of imprisonment in the surrounds of Newmarket for quite a period during which he was allowed to ride and exercise daily, but a recent writer on the period, Charles Spencer, never mentions Newmarket and says he was shuttled around.

It was King Charles II who really set Newmarket and its surrounds alight. The fun-loving King simply revelled in the place. He settled betting disputes himself and the best horseman of any monarchs of the period and rode in and won the Newmarket Town Plate in 1664. The course was a well mown grass track about four miles round, marked by tall white stakes and a flag marking the winning post.

In his excellent book Richard Onslow writes how Charles would sit for hours at the top of Warwick hill watching the horses in work. He was truly one of the earlier 'touts'. Charles II also conducted numerous affairs, finding the surrounds of Newmarket much more to his liking than Westminster. He paid his last visit there in 1684, having truly established it as the leading centre of horseracing in the country.

Queen Anne was the next monarch to patronise Newmarket and as Richard Onslow wrote, on her death in August 1714, the town found itself facing a period in which it was no more important than it had been prior to the arrival of King James I in 1605.

There is little doubt that the arrival of the Jockey Club, who became increasingly influential in the area from 1750 onwards did more for Newmarket than Royal patronage and today the Club owns much of the land where horses exercise and both its current flat courses (a National Hunt course was discontinued early in the twentieth century).

So how is Newmarket faring today? There is no doubt its importance to the industry as far as the training of horses is concerned is enormous. The town and its surrounds are still the main centre for training horses and the area also has many famous studs including the National Stud, now owned by the Jockey Club.

It is the courses which are causing concern. The Rowley Mile course only comes alive for the two Guineas days. As another commentator has stated the course was laid out as a test of the horse rather than with spectator comfort in mind and its latest grandstand has had a very mixed reception.

The Summer or July course is still a delightful place to spend an afternoons racing. The trouble is not enough people seem to agree with me. Fewer racegoers are going, unless there is a concert, when the course is packed. The average attendance is low for courses which have numerous Pattern races. The experience of being at the Rowley Mile course on a day where six Group One races were run in front of an apathetic crowd of about twelve thousand is not one which I would like to experience every day.

The course naturally gets a lot of attention at the top level of the Jockey Club and the current managing director, Amy Starkey, is very highly regarded.

Goodwood is a very popular course and is one still attracting people in large numbers. The course was laid out by the third Duke of Richmond on his own land and one would have to say that racecourse experts might do things rather differently if the course was built today. However variation in tracks is popular with the public and whilst the ups and downs suit some horses more than others, it all adds up to exciting racing.

One of the real attractions to the public is that it is owned by a popular and old, aristocratic family who have been more successful than many in keeping the public onside. I have been fortunate to stay with the Earl of March and spend a day in the Richmond box when Clement Freud was another guest. The pictures in Goodwood House are stunning with two Stubbs and two Canalettos to the fore. Both famous artists spent years as guests of the Dukes of Richmond, who recognised their talent at an early age. At the dinner party, the night I stayed, Lord March said that his eldest son had slid down the banisters the day before, crashing into a valuable antique and written off over a hundred thousand pounds in value. I thought very understandingly, he also said that children had to have some freedom in a house full of valuables!

The family has certainly looked after their racecourse and the five-day Goodwood Festival is one of the most popular in racing. I now go with George Baker and stay in great comfort with his mother. The Turf Club and the Trainers car parks for picnics add to the pleasures of the meeting. I have also been lucky to see Frankel at close quarters in the saddling enclosure, as George, who knows the layout like the back of his hand, made sure we got the best possible view of the greatest flat racehorse I have ever seen.

Goodwood has only two Group One races, the Sussex and Nassau Stakes, and six Group Twos, which include the Goodwood Cup, one of the leading long distance races in the calendar. It has other Pattern races and whilst its profits are not disclosed they must be considerable. Whilst Lord March chairs the racecourse their chief executive, Rob Fabricus, is an older, very experienced chief executive and, like York, the course is very well run.

Epsom is the home of the Derby and Oaks. The venue of the Derby was decided by the toss of a coin between Lord Derby and Sir Charles Bunbury. Bunbury's consolation prize was that he did have the winner of the first staging of the race over a mile in 1779. The race was to become the most famous in the world and famous winners decorate the honours board. In the nineteenth century they included the Flying Dutchman and Voltigeur. West Australian was the first horse to win the much coveted treble or triple crown of the 2000 Guineas, Derby and

St Leger, now almost impossible to win because of the lack of top-class stayers. Ormonde was a truly remarkable horse, never beaten in his sixteen race career and supreme over distances from seven furlongs to a mile and three-quarters. Persimmon was the first Royal winner for the Prince of Wales, later King Edward VII. In the twentieth century, Hyperion was a memorable winner for Lord Derby in 1933, the year of my birth. I must be one of the few people alive to see the great man when he came to visit my grandmother in 1943, though all I got was a patronising wave. After World War II, Tulyar 1952, Never Say Die 1954 and Sea Bird 1965 were all great horses, the last named in particular was to win the Arc by six lengths and his rating remained the highest recorded until 2012, when Frankel surpassed it.

Sir Ivor in 1968 was another exceptional horse as were Nijinsky and Mill Reef, 1970 and 1971 and of course Shergar who disappeared so mysteriously. Nijinsky by Northern Dancer, won the triple crown but his exertions in the St Leger probably cost him the Arc. Mill Reef was only beaten twice in fourteen starts, once by Brigadier Gerard. The Minstrel in 1977 was Robert Sangster's first Derby winner and a very exciting one for me as I was one of a handful of his guests at a much prized table at Epsom's out-of-date, old stand. Galileo and High Chaparral, 2001 and 2002, have both become successful stallions, particularly the first named. Sea the Stars, 2009, was a particularly exciting winner and the 2014 winner, Australia, could be anything! Now Golden Horn is another high class horse.

The greatest winning jockey is undoubtedly Lester Piggott, who won the race nine times. I will never forget his ride on Roberto, though under current whip rules he would or should have got at least a month's suspension. The unluckiest loser I have seen was Dancing Brave, who proved that sticking loyally to a stable jockey does not always pay and I was at Robert Sangster's side when he made the annoying remark to Prince Khalid Abdullah immediately after the race, 'Bad luck Khalid, that's racing.' His Highness was not a happy man!

The Oaks is now run on a Sunday, so I never go, though I did when it was on a weekday. I am also on the side of those who regretted the Derby being run on a Saturday. It used to be a great day in the national calendar like the Melbourne Cup, the nation nearly came to a standstill. Now it is just one of our Saturday's many attractions.

The Oaks is a classic, first won, appropriately, by Lord Derby's Bridget in 1779, so the two tosses of the coin each won an inaugural classic. Whilst La Fleche 1891 won sixteen of her starts, the most famous winner was Sceptre, an incomparable filly who won four classics and was second in the Derby. She was regularly ridden rather than boxed to her races and must have had incredible stamina and had she had a less fearless, gambling owner than Robert Slevier, her record would have been even more incredible. Pretty Polly, 1904, was probably the best winner until Sun Chariot in 1942, Meld, 1955 and Petite Etoile in 1959. Ouija Board in 2004 is the dam of Australia and has a fantastic future as a brood mare for the current Lord Derby. Snow Fairy, 2010, was another very good, recent winner.

Epsom's only other Group I, the Coronation Cup, has had a stream of top-class winners including Rainbow Quest, who made no mistake as a four-year-old.

As other commentators before me have said, no designer of a racecourse today would ever come up with a course like Epsom. Laid out in 1872, in the shape of a horseshoe, the start is a steep incline before quickly turning right, then runners cut the corner before moving to the left of the course sharply uphill until a hundred yards before the mile mark at which point the course is over forty yards above the start. The course is flat for over two furlongs before a sharp turn left before Tattenham corner, the home straight being adversely cambered and quite a sharp decent until the last half furlong, where the ground rises a little before the winning post.

The one great winning Derby trainer I have been lucky enough to have in depth conversations about the Derby with was Vincent O'Brien, who tried to reciprocate the conditions as closely as possible at Ballydoyle. He considered that Chester provided the best Derby trials and my powers of persuasion must have been better than I thought because following a visit from myself and Richard Thomas to the Curragh, Aidan O'Brien (no relation) has run many of his best horses in both of Chester's Derby trials, the Vase and Dee Stakes, though the Pattern Committee have, in their wisdom (or lack of it), demoted the latter race from a Group 3 to a Listed race.

Epsom is a fantastic racecourse for three days a year, the amenities are enormously improved and the current stand is first class, though I miss the old stand built by Sir Robert McAlpine and Sons who took the best box on the course and held on to it until it was demolished.

Chester is the oldest course in the country. The almost flat bowl, known as the Roodee, was the centre of sporting activities back in the mists of time (certainly in Roman times) but the decision to have horse racing was made by its mayor in 1512, though the first recorded races were a few years later about 1539. Chester has had its ups and downs, racing continuously for four hundred and seventy-five years. Surprisingly all those years later it is the most profitable flat course amongst those who announce their results and also has the third highest and occasionally second highest average attendance of any flat course. Only Ascot, and sometimes York, are ahead in this respect.

Because it is the tightest flat circuit in the country, the viewing is probably the best of any racecourse and that has certainly contributed to its popularity. The network of bars and places to eat has been carefully thought out and there is now an upmarket pub, open seven days a week, put not far from the Weighing Room. Although it is supposed to be imperative in sprint races to obtain a low draw, the management has tried, by bringing in fresh ground, to make it more possible to win from an outside draw and last season two outside runners came first and second in a two-year-old sprint. The important thing is for jockeys not to go too wide on the turn and patiently wait for gaps to open up in the short straight.

Because Chester makes so much money it is able to increase prize money and for two seasons has had a minimum of ten thousand pounds a race. When the Dee Stakes got demoted the course added another ten thousand pounds to the prize money. In fact the lack of Pattern races has meant the course doesn't have to finance them and this has greatly contributed to the profits as a result.

The main reason for the lack of Pattern has been Chester's proximity to the town centre, which in the nineteenth century and well into the twentieth led to the clamour from various clerical groups for it to be closed down. In 1856 a William Wilson led a campaign against the course which he asserted brought drunkenness, brawling, gambling, theft, prostitution, loathsome diseases, lunacy, suicide and damnation to the city.

The course was saved by Alderman Brown, who outflanked the anti-racing lobby by agreeing to a short lease and one meeting a year, although opposition continued until close to the Second World War. However, although the course continued to race, its lack of fixtures, apart from the May meeting, caused problems because when new fixtures were agreed they did not include Pattern, i.e. top-class, races.

Part of the course's problems with its critics were the enormous crowds generated. In 1886, 100,000 were said to have attended Cup day and certainly just after the two World Wars, Cup day in 1920 drew a crowd of 96,000 and in 1946, 104,000. The first Sunday meeting at the course drew over 50,000, during my time as chairman, with the Dean of Chester as a guest. Times have certainly changed!

Over the years the course has been supported by leading aristocrats in the area perhaps more fun loving than the clerical opposition. The Duke of Westminster was the first Chester Racecourse Company chairman and his influence helped to save the course and my predecessor, Lord

Leverhulme, did an enormous amount for it. The board now has an excellent chairman, and in my biased opinion, the best racecourse chief executive, who has just won an award as Chester Businessman of the year. It looks all set for another four hundred plus years!

Virtually all the Saturday meetings that follow the May Festival can expect a crowd of around twenty-five thousand. The attendance figure is the envy of most other courses but it does have its downside, namely the drunkenness which can occur at the end of the meetings. Whilst most racecourses suffer this to some extent, and I am told Newmarket High Street suffers particularly after concerts at the end of racing – but nobody seems to mind. It is particularly relevant to Chester where the course is close to the town and thousands of racegoers pour into its streets after racing. This is welcome news to those who want to attract them but it is the opposite to traders who have no interest in them. The course is well aware of the problem and has tried to act on all sensible police suggestions. The policy of allowing racegoers to bring alcohol onto the course has been severely curtailed.

Sandown Park is London's most attractive racecourse and, since the closure of Hurst Park, stands alone in this respect. It did not start racing until 1875 and was fortunate to gain royal patronage immediately. The Prince of Wales (later Edward VII) attended the second meeting and his filly, Counterpane, was to be his first flat winner, with the result that Sandown enjoyed royal patronage from then onwards.

More recently it was a course very popular with the Queen Mother, who saw a thrilling victory of her horse, Special Cargo, who got up in the last stride to win the Whitbread Gold Cup in 1984 and she attended meetings there every year until her death at the age of 102.

The amenities at Sandown are excellent and I have been a regular racegoer there from an early age. I particularly enjoyed the Whitbread meeting, where I regularly went with Ernie Harrison and Eric Parker. Although I have had many runners there, the only notable success I can remember was with Rollahead, who won a Group 3 race there. I have had a runner in the course's only Group I race, the Eclipse Stakes, Cormorant Wood, which was a disaster, the ground being far too firm for the filly.

The twenty Pattern races put a strain on the course's finances and it is yet another course where the racing public should be pleased the Jockey Club stands behind it. Indeed it is one of the Jockey Club's most attractive flat courses. It also has an equally good National Hunt course, where attendances often exceed the flat ones. The layout of the fences jumped at great speed make for a particularly good viewing.

Haydock Park is another excellent dual purpose track. Haydock, for some reason I cannot fathom, does not attract anywhere near the crowds of Chester, although it is much nearer the cities of Liverpool and Manchester and is close to the M6, which comes to within a mile of its boundaries.

It now has one Group I race, the Haydock Sprint Cup, over six furlongs and a total of thirteen Pattern races. It also has an excellent National Hunt course, although the change from 'drop' fences to normal, at the end of the far straight, is not popular with many supporters.

Owned for a lengthy period by the Whittle family, the course is now firmly under Jockey Club control. It boasts one of the most attractive paddocks in the country. It has long been a favourite of mine and when I had flat horses I often ran them there – with varied success. I do remember a fast two-year-old called Oswestry Covert, winning when I was certain she was beaten but the angle favours the stand side in a tight finish. Another winner I well remember was Zip Fastener, who won the Victor Ludorum Hurdle for four-year-olds, then a good preparatory race for the Triumph Hurdle. Sadly the same horse had to be put down when about to come third in a hurdle but he had put his foot in a divot from a previous race. In both cases Fred Rimell was the trainer and on the first occasion he had to rush down to try and placate the owners of an unplaced horse behind Zip Fastener. He did not succeed, the perils of running two horses in a race!

The course has good facilities although the owners and trainers bar and restaurant are not on the same level as Chester's. Lord Daresbury is now the chairman and, having been highly successful at Aintree, sees one of his main aims to get the attendance higher. Bill Whittle still comes to most meetings and plays an excellent 'elder statesman' role.

Doncaster, historically one of the oldest courses in the country and a really first-class track, is now owned by ARC and is certainly their 'Jewel in the Crown' being the home of Britain's oldest classic, the St Leger. This race was first run in 1776 devised by Anthony St Leger, an army officer and politician who lived near Doncaster. It was initially referred to as 'A Sweepstake of 25 Guineas', and its original distance was two miles. The rules stipulated that colts and geldings were to carry 8 st, and fillies would receive an allowance of 2 lb.

The inaugural running was held at Cantley Common on 24 September 1776. The first winner was an unnamed filly owned by the event's organiser, the 2nd Marquess of Rockingham. The filly was later named Allabaculia.

The title St Leger Stakes was decided at a dinner party held in

1777 to discuss the following year's race. It was suggested that it should be called the Rockingham Stakes in honour of the host, the Marquess of Rockingham, but the Marquess proposed that it should be named instead after Anthony St Leger who had devised it. The event was moved to its present location, Town Moor, in 1778.

The race came to national prominence in 1800, when a horse called Champion registered the first Derby-St Leger double. Its length was cut to 1 mile, 6 furlongs and 193 yards in 1813, and despite some minor alterations has remained much the same ever since. The victory of West Australian in 1853 completed the first success in the Triple Crown. The course comes alive twice a year, on the first day of the flat season, when the Lincoln is now run there, and the St Leger meeting in September.

Like Chester and York, Doncaster can trace racing as far back as the end of the sixteenth century, though the current course, Town Moor, only came into play in 1710. The September fixture has been continuous since 1751.

The track is basically flat and has a sharp left turn out of the straight before a straight run of about a mile. A gradual bend of five furlongs then turns back into the home straight, which is just short of five furlongs. Races of up to a mile can be run on the straight course. The National Hunt course follows the flat and because of the general flat nature of the whole course, the fences are often jumped at considerable speed.

Doncaster was the scene of one of my setbacks, when Precipice Wood came fourth in the St Leger. In my opinion he should have been much nearer the winner and sadly his excellent trainer and I were both too inexperienced to know that an unexpectedly top-class horse needed a stronger jockey.

Newbury, is a most attractive dual purpose course and one of my favourites, where I had many successful (and some less so) days. David Marchwood, one of my racing friends, and I used to go there when I was in my twenties and I well remember being his guest (he was then the youngest ever director of Schweppes) at the two-mile hurdle in February, then sponsored by his company.

When I was co-founder of Haynes Hanson and Clark, we started a race at Newbury, the Haynes Hanson and Clark Stakes. This has now been run for over thirty years and we are easily their oldest sponsors. In our time we have had three Derby winners and a number of very good horses win the race. The conditions have changed over the years and it is no longer for unraced horses or for maidens, with the result that recent runnings have not thrown up such top-class horses.

Like Chester, Newbury is owned by its shareholders and for a period both courses had the same partner of a famous firm of stockbrokers dealing with the share transactions of the two companies. Recently some land has been sold for housing which has given the course a healthy injection of cash. The board of directors is particularly strong with a leading businessman as their chairman and two very rich, successful people, Eric Penser and Lady Lloyd Webber, on the board. Julian Thick (who the Jockey Club surprisingly let go), is the chief executive.

Newbury has one Group I race, the Lockinge, in which my great filly, Cormorant Wood, dead heated for first place, although it was short of her ideal distance. The trophy was of a mare and foal by Philip Blacker, to be held by the winner for twelve months (in my case six). I liked it so much I commissioned a replica from Philip. There are twenty-one other Pattern races.

The National Hunt course is particularly suited to chasers and Newbury has not made the fences quite as easy as some other courses. The meetings are often better attended than the flat. Two big races which are often won by good horses are the Hennessey Gold Cup and the two-mile handicap hurdle in early February, recently sponsored by Betfair.

Anybody who tried, as I have, to get home on a Friday night can understand why attendances on a Friday are so sparse. It took John Gosden and I four-and-a-half hours to get to Newmarket and Cheshire respectively.

It will be interesting to see what effect the present housing development has on the course and car parks. The surrounds to the course are part of Newbury's charm but we shall only know the answer when the developments are finished. The A34 bypass took an enormous amount of traffic away from the town but because many racegoers have to journey back along busy roads, Fridays are particularly difficult and the course has poor attendances on them. As I have already said, the board, headed by Dominic Burke, is particularly strong and the course is expertly managed.

Although **Kempton** is a well-functioning course it has none of the charm of Sandown nearby or the now defunct Hurst Park adjacent. It still has its big day, the King George VI Chase on Boxing day which is one of the big three-mile chases of the season, and I remember with pleasure my National Hunt mare, One Gulp, winning some black type there. It is, however, home to a barrage of all-weather fixtures, which trainers tell me can be a good introduction for young flat and National Hunt horses. Whilst it is a premier all-weather track, the meetings are poorly attended and an average attendance would be meaningless. It does, I am told, have very profitable car boot sales and the course is generally well run.

Ayr, once a top-class racecourse and the only course in Scotland to have Group races, has been beset with boardroom strife in recent years which has weakened its finances. I used to go there with Robert Sangster in the sixties and early seventies and we stayed at Turnberry and played golf. Robert was amazed how strong its betting market was in those days but I confess I haven't been in recent years. The two big days are the Ayr Gold Cup, a handicap sprint on the flat, and the Scottish Grand National over jumps and run shortly after the Aintree festival. Totally different to Aintree, the jumps are very soft and jumped at great speed. The day also has the Scottish Champion Hurdle, which I won with River Ceiriog, in the eighties. Again I never remember a horse of mine jumping hurdles at greater speed.

Ayr's history can be traced back to the sixteenth century but its present track only commenced in 1901; the jumps course dates back to 1950.

These then are the top 'lucky 13' racecourses in my book but the degrees of luck I've had at each of them vary enormously.

Queen Anne, founder of Royal Ascot.

Royal Ascot 1897, Royal Enclosure in the foreground.

A wonderful print of the old paddock at Ascot with all the trees and foliage on a hot summer's afternoon. How different from today's!

My grandfather's horse winning a chase at Newbury.

Two of my grandfather's racehorses on a foggy day in North Wales.

A picture of Chester racecourse by Peter Smith. Richard Thomas and I are in the foreground.

Chester Chairman welcoming Prince and Princess Michael of Kent on a visit to the racecourse.

Self with Joe Coral after winning his sponsored race at Newbury 1975.

Precipice Wood (J LIndley) after winning Ascot Gold Cup, Royal Ascot 1970.

Precipice Wood by Sarah Ponsonby.

Presentation by Nick Robinson at the TBA awards ceremony on successive years to celebrate Precipice Wood, Champion National Hunt Stallion.

Presentation by Charles Morrison at the TBA awards ceremony.

Charles and Rose Lowther, Willy and Caroline Jenks and myself with Sadler's Wells at Coolmore.

River Ceiriog after winning the Supreme Novice at Cheltenham at 40/1. Nicky Henderson's first winner at the festival.

Self with Steve Cauthen after winning the B&H Gold Cup (now Juddmonte) on Cormorant Wood at York, defeating Sadler's Wells, who started favourite. Doug Francis's head can just be seen between us.

Cormorant Wood after winning the Juddmonte.

Cormorant Wood after winning Champion Stakes by T.S. La Fontaine. The artist had never visited Newmarket before I asked him to go there and considerable artist's licence has been used!

Presentation after Cormorant Wood wins the Benson and Hedges International, York.

Cormorant Wood after winning the Benson and Hedges at York.

Hunter Chaser, Compton Lad.

Haynes, Hanson & Clark Stakes, Newbury, 21st running of the race. Anthony Hanson, Nick Clark, myself and wives.

Presenting trophies to Stan Mellor and Philip Blacker, McAlpine day at Bangor-on-Dee.

Marieson, ridden by Anthony Johnson.

Star of Screen (Tom Morgan), winner of the Eider Chase, Newcastle.

A memorial race gathering of Robert Sangster's closest friends at Newmarket.

My brother Billy, who took a half share in Marnrack, my first racehorse.

Robert Sangster with one of hundreds of racing trophies.

Doug Francis, my near neighbour at Carden. He was a great friend and influence in the early part of my life and was best man at my second wedding.

Cartoon by Mark Huskinson.

Chapter 9

Middle Age

After the wonderful era of Precipice Wood and other lesser but fun horses the seventies were disappointing for me. Whilst I continued to support Rosemary Lomax her marriage situation had deteriorated and I had a new trainer, Barry Hills and another Robert Sangster had introduced me to, Jeremy Hindley. Robert had a number of horses with Barry and a few with Jeremy, who was to train my best horse of that era, Coed Cochion. He was Precipice Wood's half brother but had a crooked leg which enabled us to buy him cheaply, though the leg didn't stop him running well for over two seasons. Jeremy was by far the richest trainer I ever had but was a very complex man. He was educated at Winchester which produced pupils who followed the school motto – manners maketh man – but who also tended to be intellectually ahead of the products of other public schools. Jeremy's manners were fine and he was very personable but he did have a touch of arrogance and what nobody but himself realised was that he was an alcoholic. Nobody in the period I trained with him could really define an alcoholic. We all drank far too much, Robert, Barry and myself, and I just assumed he was similar to the three of us. Charles Benson, a great friend of all of us, particularly Robert, was another, though he developed diabetes at about this period which was the first medical problem any of us had.

My first year with Jeremy as a trainer was made difficult with his insistence that his stable jockey, Tony Kimberley, was top-class but had not had the opportunities. By this time I had learnt the difference between a very good jockey and an ordinary one and to me Kimberley was definitely in the second category. Jeremy would have none of it and at the Chester May meeting Coed Cochion was beaten having looked likely to win. Jeremy said, 'He threw that away,' and I, thinking he meant Kimberley not the horse, said, 'I agree it wasn't his finest ride.' I then received a torrent of abuse about being a bad loser. The fact was that Coed Cochion was no more suited to Chester than Precipice Wood who did win a small race there but by a far lesser margin than he should have done. They were both strong galloping horses who were suited to a lengthy flat track. Coed Cochion did win the Coral Autumn Cup at Newbury and we looked forward to a good season as a four-year-old. We had decided Coed Cochion needed a pacemaker and Jeremy found me a partner in a rich Omani owner who not only took a half share in Coed Cochion but insisted on paying for all of the pacemaker. We entered both for a nice long distance race in France only to see the pacemaker run out and Coed Cochion run poorly in a slowly run race. The next race was the Ascot Stakes and we started favourite with Paul Cook aboard. I have already alluded to this in another chapter but the pacemaker started off happily and about half way had a long lead with the rest of the field well behind. Coming up the hill before the straight Cook realised that he had to make a move but he had left it far too late and given Coed Cochion far too much to do. The pacemaker was a comfortable winner at 66/1 and we finished third. It transpired later that Lester Piggott may have influenced the result as on an unfancied horse he had apparently shouted half way that they were going much too fast.

Mindful of the rocket I had received from Jeremy at Chester, I shook the Omani's hand and tried to look cheerful, though I was horrified, as was Jeremy. Paul Cook took considerable stick from the press for not making an effort sooner and determined to gain some consolation we went for the Queen Alexandra at two and three-quarter miles, the longest race on the calendar. I told Paul Cook firmly that he was to give the horse every chance and he rode an excellent race winning decisively though this was the second hard race of the week, and although he didn't break down, the crooked leg led to honourable retirement. We should have had the Ascot Stakes/Queen Alexandra double. Such is racing!

Jeremy was the first of us all to discover the delights of Barbados. As mentioned in the Sangster chapter, he originally bought a house in a small village about a mile and a half from the beach, which in those days had Greensleeves as the main tourist hotel. He did have a beach house and eventually got planning permission to convert it into a large house and after I had one holiday at his house in the village we moved to his enlarged beach house. I have to say that the house in the village had a lot of charm, there was a pond with a mass of noisy frogs and at night monkeys would arrive on the roof. The monkeys never really bothered us the way they did at the Dattai Hotel in Thailand years later, where they could be quite a pest. Barbados itself was also wonderful when Jeremy first discovered it. He was to be joined by a host of billionaires, millionaires and extremely rich and generally nice people but the island got more and more expensive as it prospered and, to me, lost the charm I had first found in Jeremy's house in the village.

Jeremy, like me, fell in love with life in South Africa or rather the Cape, as he never made his home anywhere else, first living in the suburbs of Cape Town and then moving to Hermanus where tragically, having developed Motor Neurone Disease, he finally passed away.

My other two main trainers, Barry Hills and John Edwards over jumps, had winners for me if not big ones and it was not until the early eighties that I was to hit the jackpot again on the flat for the second time.

Cormorant Wood was bred out of a staying mare, Quarry Wood, by a stallion I had selected, Home Guard who Vincent O'Brien had taken me to see at Ballydoyle. He was next to his full brother who was a better racehorse but I fell in love with Home Guard who was an enormous, imposing horse with, according to Vincent, a wonderful temperament unlike his brother who Vincent had found to be 'a real handful' – his words, not mine. Quarry Wood had won four small races, the one I remember best a mile and three-quarter race at Redcar. I have a photograph of myself, my first wife, Jane, and eldest son, Euan, a schoolboy, to prove it. The other memorable race of the filly was the Chester Cup where Pat Rohan, who trained her, insisted on putting up a favoured apprentice who when he saw he was not going to be in the first three dropped his hands and allowed fourth place to slip away. Fourth places had just been given prize money and the look on the lad's smiling face vanished when I said 'Didn't you know there is a prize for fourth place?' With hindsight she had come into the straight full of running and plainly had not really stayed the two-and-a-quarter miles at Chester. In other words she wasn't an out and out stayer. This turned out to be very important as Barry Hills and I were both convinced that Cormorant Wood would stay a minimum of a mile and a half.

Barry didn't hurry her at two and she had two small races, winning the second over seven furlongs at Leicester comfortably. At that time all we were thinking about were the big races over a mile and a half at three. The fact that the filly might not stay that trip never occurred to either of us. As a result we started with the Lingfield Derby Trial as her first race. When the day came the weather was foul and the race was actually run on heavy ground. She finished second with Steve Cauthen on board and we were all mildly disappointed. If we had known then what we knew at the end of the year it was of course an incredible achievement to finish second in a Group race over a mile and a half on heavy ground. The Oaks seemed to be the obvious next race and Steve was unavailable to ride her for reasons I cannot really remember. I did not have a retainer (he was retained for Barry by Robert Sangster) and

Barry booked the great Lester, the only time he was ever to ride for me. Epsom was at its hottest on Oaks day and we had a very good lunch with Nick Robinson who I had asked to join us. Nick and I watched the race together and the combination seemed in great shape after Tattenham Corner only to fade in the last two furlongs with Lester dropping his hands about a hundred yards from the finish and failing to get fourth place which was worth eight thousand and some black type at stud. I was incandescent with fury and asked Nick to come out with me. Lester looked his usual inscrutable self and I said, 'Couldn't you have been fourth?' with which he put his head back and bayed with laughter. Not many people have seen Lester laugh and my sense of humour by this time was non-existent. Barry was nowhere in sight and Nick tried to defuse the situation by saying she didn't have a hard race so perhaps it's for the best in the long run. The really serious thing was that he didn't tell us the filly didn't stay and that was to cost me a small fortune later.

As a result we ran her again in the Prince of Wales over a mile and a half and again she didn't stay the trip. We decided to give her a break and come back later in the summer with the Virginia Stakes, a valuable race at Newcastle, the selected race for the return over a mile and a quarter. Barry had a runner in America with Steve on board and the arrangement was that we should use a private plane from Heathrow and pick me up at my company's own airstrip near Wrexham. All that went well and although I did think both Barry and Steve showed signs of wear and tear we headed happily for Newcastle. The race had cut up to three runners because the odds-on favourite had frightened off the opposition. The race could not have gone better. We sailed past the odds-on favourite and decided to go for the Sun Chariot, then a Group Two for fillies at Newmarket. I had a business trip to South Africa and came back just before the Sun Chariot, again over a mile and a quarter, which we won less easily but still comfortably.

As she was entered for the Champion Stakes we decided to have a go, though we all felt that we were probably aiming too high. The day of the race was one of the windiest I ever remember and the decision to land on Newmarket's grass strip was not the cleverest either (I always flew to Cambridge afterwards). However we made it safely though with a few bumps and Doug and Richard Francis who had come with us, Angela and I, Barry and Penny, all had lunch. None of us really fancied the filly and we all made for our usual place to watch races at Newmarket – the end of the members' stand just above the rails bookies with the finishing line eighty yards further on. Cormorant Wood was last three furlongs out when she began to weave through the field. As she passed us she was still not in front and it was impossible to tell whether she had won or not. Barry had already made for the exit and the first person I saw was Christie Grimthorpe, the father of Prince Khalid's racing manager. 'I don't think you've won,' said Christie, 'and there is a lot of interference.' I went out to lead the filly in and said to Steve, who by this time had been announced the winner, 'Did you interfere with anybody?' 'Only one who finished well back,' he replied, 'so I don't think we are in any trouble.' The stewards' enquiry seemed to go on for ever but an announcement came that the winner was not involved in the enquiry and I tried to comb my hair for the forthcoming presentation. This proved impossible as the gale had increased and I received the magnificent trophy from Sheik Hamdan with my hair almost obliterating my face. I have described the race in my chapter on jockeys. I can only repeat that to see one of the greatest world class jockeys of all time riding one's horse to victory in one of the toughest races on the British calendar is a thrill like no other. We flew back to Manchester and Doug Francis drove us back to Swettenham. Fortunately we didn't run into any police as he weaved his way back!

We then received an invitation to run in the Arlington Million, an international race in Washington over a mile and a half. In my state of euphoria I agreed to accept knowing that All Along, a useful French filly, would be running and because we had finished so strongly at Newmarket we still thought she would stay a mile and a half. I also agreed to pay for Barry, Penny and Steve to go on the Concorde Washington flight at my expense and for us all to stay in the best hotel in Washington. The whole exercise cost a fortune and the filly ran a similar race to the Oaks, well there two out she faded to sixth in the last two furlongs. At least we now got some valuable information from the jockey that she didn't stay a mile and a half. It had cost me a lot of money to find this out!

We entered the 1984 season with that knowledge and her first run was in the Lockinge (now a Group I) at Newbury over a mile where we dead-heated for first place with Wasil, an Arab-owned horse of John Dunlop's. We went for the Queen Anne at Royal Ascot, also over a mile and came third with Steve telling us that she wouldn't stride out on the very fast ground and in her next race, the Eclipse, he was even more outspoken, 'She just won't have this ground.'

Between the last two races I had sold the filly for 1.3 million dollars with the proviso that I kept a half share for her racing career but the purchaser could purchase the other half share when she retired from racing. I did not know that she would run another amazing race in the Benson and Hedges International Stakes (now the Juddmonte) when she pulverised a top-class field with Sadler's Wells, the favourite, fourth and Tolomeo much further behind than in the Champion Stakes. Steve Cauthen had again ridden her brilliantly seeing that she was going so easily coming into York's long straight he dropped her back a few places so he could get an unimpeded run. Great credit must also go to Barry Hills as in a firm ground summer she had not been easy to train.

I had had an insurance bet on her knowing that if she won the race I had sold her too cheaply and I still have the video of John McCririck saying 'The bookmakers have had a field day, except for poor Michael Simmonds who has laid a silly bet,' and the camera switches to Michael Simmons of Heathorns who is literally tearing his hair out having laid me 40,000 to 2,000 knowing I was having an insurance bet – easily the most money I have won on a horse, but still far short of what I had lost on the sale. She broke down the following day, her stud career was disappointing although she did produce Rockhopper, who won seven Group races though not a Group One. Although I would have received far more after the Benson and Hedges International I had one consolation in that the dollar was almost on a par with the pound, which was never to happen again.

Quarry Wood was to produce a second good horse in River Ceiriog. Unfortunately he had a set-back with Barry Hills but Steve Cauthen thought he was a Group horse in the making. He did not come back into training until a four-year-old, when I sent him to Nick Henderson to go hurdling. Prior to Cheltenham he had run twice showing some promise and I insisted Nicky enter him for the Supreme Novice, which he did with some misgivings. When it came to declaring him, Nicky wanted to go for a minor race but I insisted on his making the declaration. In the event we were very lucky to get in the race, the final declarations were right on the maximum, and with little form, we might well have been balloted out. On the day of the race I had a board meeting at Stafford for Hall Engineering, and then set off for Cheltenham, where Nicky, Angela, who had got a lift, and I were all meeting for lunch. I wanted to have a decent bet but Nicky told me to save it for our runner on the Saturday, Baby Sigh, at Wolverhampton. I did have a hundred each way at forty-to-one and went out to watch the race. River Ceiriog was one of the easiest winners I have ever had; he had the race won down the far side and nothing got near him. The race sponsored by Waterford Glass yielded me sixty-nine magnificent tumblers and wine glasses and a tremendous trophy. Both Nicky and I have the trophies in our dining rooms, his being overshadowed by three Champion hurdle ones.

The next race was the big Novice Hurdle at Aintree where Nicky and Steve Smith Eccles thought that victory was a formality. I was less confident as the trip was two furlongs further and I remembered how quickly Cormorant Wood had stopped beyond the mile and a quarter mark. All my fears were borne out and although Steve blamed himself for being over confident I still think the horse's stamina gave out. The race had a dramatic sequel as Steve, furious at the reversal, stayed up drinking after his girlfriend, Di Haine, went to bed and got locked out of his room in the process. He went back to his car to sleep and woke up to find he was being driven down the M6 motorway. The two thieves abandoned the car and ran to the verge to leave Steve to drive back to the hotel. History does not relate what sort of welcome he received from Di but very unwisely he gave an interview to BBC television. His only ride on the Friday was on my horse, Baby Sigh, who had been beaten at odds-on just after Cheltenham and stood no chance but he had some fancied rides on the Saturday, including the Grand National favourite and the owners were none too pleased about the Thursday night revelry, particularly when his National mount fell early in the race.

His last race of the season was the Scottish Champion Hurdle at Ayr where Steve led from start to finish and we all looked forward to running a fresh horse in big races the following season. The first chosen was a valuable hurdle at Windsor which looked an easy race but he finished a modest third and the following day a virus was discovered which virtually put him out for the rest of the season. As in Precipice Wood's case, the regular scoping which takes place now would probably have uncovered the virus but, unlike Precipice Wood, River Ceiriog was never in my opinion quite as good again. He did run in the Champion Hurdle as Nicky's second string to See You Then out for a hat trick of wins and as Steve Smith Eccles was obviously on See You Then I persuaded Nicky to put up Dermot Brown who had ridden my good hunter-chaser Compton Lad. Although Dermot's riding career ended in shame and ignominy, I have no complaints on the ride he gave River Ceiriog. He led briefly at the second last and fell at the last but for which he would have finished third or fourth. Again I blamed stamina deficiency for the result.

River Ceiriog had only one more race, a steeplechase where Smith Eccles, having made an amazing partial recovery, pulled him up. His tendons had gone and he was given away to go hunting.

I did have two other good flat horses. Rollahead was bought by Jeremy Hindley for me one bright Autumn morning at Newmarket. We were having a late breakfast when Micky Suffolk (Earl of) approached us and said he was acting for Bill Sterling who was the breeder and would like to buy a half share back. I had met Bill a few times in South Africa where his company, Sterling Astaldi, were competitors of ours and had found him pleasant company and so agreed, with some reluctance, to sell him a half share. I never saw Bill again and when Rollahead started racing a small group which included Micky and William Pigott Brown were usually present. Rollahead won at the Chester May meeting and looked like winning the listed Woodcote Stakes on Derby day. Several lengths clear at the distance he got unbalanced and was caught near the finish. We went to Royal Ascot where, despite getting loose at the start of the Windsor Castle, he was remounted and won comfortably. He won again at Sandown but only finished second in a Group Two, his final race for me. Joe Mercer, his regular jockey, whispered in my ear, 'He's getting clever governor; he should have won.' Jeremy and I agreed we should sell him at the end of the season and give him one more race in the Royal Lodge. Micky was told what we were planning and came back with an offer from some character in Yorkshire nobody had ever heard of. I had to go into the Westminster hospital with a severe attack of my skin problem – psoriasis – and was lying comfortably in my bed when Micky was led in by a nurse despite the fact that I was not supposed to have many visitors. I looked at his shirt with coronets emblazoned on it and realised being the Earl of Suffolk did have advantages. He waved a large cheque in front of me and continued with his sob story of his friend in Yorkshire being desperate for the first racehorse. I took the cheque, despite Charles Benson telling me there was trickery afoot, and the character from Yorkshire turned out to be a combination of Robert Sangster and William Pigott Brown. They benefited little from their deception as Rollahead was sent to South Africa where he accomplished little and finished as a minor stallion in Zimbabwe.

The last good flat horse I had was Free Sweater, bought jointly by Jeremy Hindley and myself and trained by Barry Hills as Jeremy had given up training. He was named by us as both of us were prolific sweaters. He showed considerable promise at two when close up in the Champagne Stakes and fourth in the Beresford Stakes in Ireland achieving a *Timeform* rating of over a hundred without reaching the first three. Our first race with him as a three-year-old was the Dee Stakes at Chester May meeting which we won reasonably convincingly and we decided to go for the Italian Derby. I combined the race with a business trip to Egypt where we were looking for contracts. Every time I went to Egypt I picked up the local bug, aptly known as Gypy Tummy. I took the Air Italia flight to Rome and stationed myself at the front of the plane intending to head the queue for the loo. To my surprise I was beaten to it by three passengers and both the pilot and co-pilot appeared separately and I realised half the flight were in the same predicament. Cairo to Rome is a short hop and I got to Rome safely and went to the excellent hotel Rocco Forte had booked me into. A light supper in my room and an early bed got me upright the next day and Angela, who had flown over with Barry and Penny, arrived and we all headed for the racecourse. It was one of the hottest days I ever remember facing and fortunately I had got the hotel to press my tropical suit I had taken to Egypt. The horse seemed fine in the paddock and Barry said, 'You won't regret turning down that offer' – the offer being £250,000 from an Italian desperate to have a runner. Several minutes later I have never regretted anything more. He went into the lead probably too early and was well beaten. Taken back to England he ran badly twice before coming second in a big handicap, the Festival of Britain Stakes at Ascot's last flat meeting of the year. He was sold for about half what Jeremy and I would have received had we taken the Italian's offer.

Chapter 10

Stewarding

I must have been the youngest racecourse steward in the country when I started at Wolverhampton in my twenties. My good racing friend at the time, Brian Jenks, was chairman of the panel and talked me into it although I pleaded I was too young and inexperienced. We had no aids other than a photo finish and had to rely on good eyesight and an expensive pair of binoculars. The one thing we had in our favour was the lack of interest the media took and our decisions were rarely queried. Of the two enquiries I remember at Wolverhampton the first concerned interference to the second by Bill Marshall's son who was apprenticed to his father. During a lengthy enquiry Brian tried to stop Bill Marshall answering continuously for his son, but with little success. It was obvious to us that his son had not kept his horse remotely straight and had seriously impeded the second. Bill finished his final oration with an impassioned plea to us, 'I am sure you gentlemen will do the right thing and let the result stand,' but sadly for him we disqualified his horse and suspended his son for ten days. The second enquiry concerned John Haine who appeared to make little effort to ride his horse out and we reported him to the Jockey Club who took his licence away for a while. Whilst I thought the decision was correct I was not sure whether someone like myself should be partly responsible for removing somebody's livelihood.

As Bangor-on-Dee was the local course it seemed natural for me to become a steward there too but the directors were concerned by my enthusiastic betting. In fact I was not wagering nearly as much as people thought, but I probably got over excited when I won. I was finally appointed to the panel and Sir Edward Hanmer, a veteran steward of long standing, gave me a lecture that one should never have a bet as a steward.

The next appointment was to become a steward at Chester, a big step up as Chester was a major course and I found myself chairman of the panel soon after the appointment and just after meeting Robert Sangster. This was the first time I was in the chair and having been to a dinner party of the Sangsters at Swettenham the night before the festival

May meeting started, I knew that they fancied their filly Shellshock considerably. To my horror Shellshock appeared to be coming to win the Group race only to be violently impeded by Geoff Lewis's horse and an enquiry was immediately announced. As I made my way to the stewards' room past the then winners enclosure, Tim Kitson said to Robert Sangster looking straight at me 'You are certain to get the race, Robert.' There were five people in the room, the three stewards, myself, Sir Guy Lowther and Pat Smyly, the manager of the Grosvenor stud, Charles Toller, the clerk of the course and Mr Christian, the senior Jockey Club stipendiary steward. We showed the two jockeys the film which to me clearly proved that Shellshock, thinking she was about to be rammed into by Geoff Lewis's mount who had veered almost at right angles towards her (he had broken his leg), had checked her run. The problem was the two horses had not actually touched although the gap between them was minute and Shellshock was left cowering on the stand rails. When I asked the two jockeys for their explanations Geoff Lewis said, 'Yes, my horse did drift a bit, but it was fast going and we never stopped Eddery riding.' (There were no Mr's in those days.) Pat Eddery, the rider of Shellshock, had just come over from South Africa and was shy and nervous, allowing Geoff Lewis to dominate the discussion.

When the jockeys left the room Pat Smyly opened the discussion. 'I saw no interference; I have no doubt the result should stand.' I later discovered he disliked Robert intensely. Mr Christian said much the same and Charles Toller who had no right to speak muttered about betting money. Guy Lowther was the only one to say that in his opinion there had been interference. I was in a nightmare situation. If I voted with Lowther, I could see I would be accused of favouring Robert and probably of having a large bet on his horse (which I hadn't). To have three experienced old hands so adamant they were right was truly frightening and in the end I took the coward's way out and sided with Smyly, Christian and Toller. Fifty years later, whilst I am sure Shellshock unimpeded would have won the race, I am not sure whether stewards today would have disqualified the winner. Nowadays it seems to me they do almost anything to let the result stand. Maybe the jury is still out.

Philip Leverhulme congratulated me on the decision but Robert was furious and Lester Piggott, who had been fined £10 for an earlier frivolous objection, poured fuel on the fire by telling him it was the worst decision he had ever seen, as did Charles Benson who had a large bet on the Sangster filly.

I still think stewarding is largely a combination of concentration and common sense. Much is routine and only very occasionally does a difficult situation arise. At Haydock, the course where I stewarded for around forty years, I can only remember a handful of difficult decisions. One was an enquiry involving a Willy Carson winner. David Wilson the chairman of the panel took stewarding very seriously, almost too seriously, I felt. George Owen, who had been drafted on the panel when the media complained too few ex trainers became stewards, was a lovely man but not decisive enough to make a good steward. I felt that any interference was marginal and wanted to let the result stand, but David Wilson was adamant we should disqualify and persuaded George to agree with him, stupidly I fell for, 'we should all be unanimous', knowing that Willy Carson, one of the best 'talkers' in the business, would be sure to appeal, which he did, and David Wilson, who represented us, lost the appeal and came back with his tail between his legs.

There were though two difficult cases at Haydock when I was in the chair. The first concerned a small popular lady trainer, Norma Macauley, whose horse we disqualified in a major sprint contest. It was a very complicated situation with three horses involved in a rough finish with the second who was awarded the race going for a narrow gap on the stand rails. We were convinced the first had seriously interfered with the second and much depended on the evidence of the third's jockey, whose testimony supported this.

The press made a real meal of it and Mrs Macauley got a lot of sympathy. At the appeal she had a very experienced solicitor, Mr Richardson, and the Jockey Club appeal panel was headed by Michael Wrigley, the father of the recent senior steward Nicholas Wrigley. I had done a lot of preparation for what I knew would be a difficult enquiry and as a 'frustrated barrister' (I had wanted to be a barrister if I had not been drafted into the family company) I now had an opportunity to conduct an interesting case. Things were going fairly evenly with the jockeys on the first two completely disagreeing with each other and when the jockey on the third started retracting his original statement I interrupted and said to him, 'I am reading your original statement at Haydock racecourse. Are you now saying you were lying?' That completely shut him up and he didn't continue his retraction. Our decision was upheld and I was asked to stay behind and Michael Wrigley said, 'We would like to congratulate you on the way you handled a really difficult case.' Possibly my finest hour as a steward!

The second case was Haydock's premier race then the Swettenham Stakes a major Group sprint, now a Group One, sponsored by Robert Sangster's stud and won by the owner, though he was elsewhere. For some time and partly due to the Shellshock enquiry at Chester, I had vowed not to get involved again in one involving my great friend, and when Lester Piggott in his come-back season objected to the first and the second I got up and said to the stipendiary, 'I think I should stand down.' He put his hands on my shoulders and said, 'You stay where you are,' and whispered, 'the others are too inexperienced.' Knowing that Robert's mother, Peggy Sangster, was going to present the trophy and grasping the furore that would ensue should the enquiry not go the winner's way, I stayed with considerable reluctance. We had the jockeys in and all seemed to go well. Brent Thompson on board the winner had been brought over from Australia by Robert and although no Steve Cauthen was competent enough, though not the strongest in a tight finish. He stated he had done nothing wrong and was strongly supported by Walter Swinburn who rode the second, both jockeys being aware that Lester Piggott was trying to gain a place on them. Lester then made his usual enigmatic statement that he had been lent on by both of them. We played the film. This showed that Lester had not been affected but that on or near the line Swinburn had been 'lent on' by Brent Thompson.

Having seen the film Swinburn began to change his story and using the same tactics as in the MacAuley case I asked the stenographer to read his statement. 'Are you now saying that you were untruthful, Mr Swinburn?' 'No sir, but the film does raise some questions.' The main one being it was difficult to tell exactly where the line was as the grass had not been cut.

Privately I had little doubt that Brent Thompson had lent on Swinburn, probably just before the finishing line, and had mentally decided if either of the other stewards wanted to disqualify I would have to agree with them. Fortunately both stewards felt that the winner should keep the race and I was spared the wrath of Peggy Sangster. The finishing line was always well mown from then onwards, but I think I probably owe Philip Arkwright, the clerk of the course, a debt of gratitude for leaving it unmown on this occasion. I rang Robert Sangster that night to tell him we were even after the Shellshock Chester inquiry but he was totally disinterested. He had moved on to loftier heights.

Although not an enquiry, the jockeys' strike at Haydock was an interesting experience which was badly handled on all sides. I was fortunately not in the chair as Charles Weatherby, who had done relatively little stewarding despite his famous name, had that privilege and Victor Gubbins, a very experienced steward, and I were the other two. As soon as I got into the stewards' room I was informed by one of the two stipendiaries that there was a problem regarding the ground. The jockeys had raced on very dubious ground some ten days earlier and were not keen to repeat the experience. On the other hand Philip Arkwright, who was very sensitive to criticism of the course, was convinced the ground was raceable and had bent Charles Weatherby's ear on the subject. We held an immediate inspection as the jockeys said the ground was unfit and I found myself with the Hills twins who were two of the jockeys' spokesmen. 'Look at this piece of ground,' one said. I had a good look and said 'It's not that bad.' 'No I meant this piece,' as they moved me to another bit of ground which again looked raceable to me. What had happened was that the ground had improved against the jockeys' expectations as the ones who had come by plane had told the pilots to get ready to go straight back. After two inspections we all agreed with Arkwright that the course was raceable but by this time we were already over the original start time for the first race. I did shout at the stipendiaries, 'Should we tell the jockeys?' only to be told, 'We haven't time,' as they headed for the weighing room where a delegation headed no doubt by the Hills twins told them that they were not riding.

Unfortunately the Jockey Club didn't hold an immediate enquiry. In fact it was months later before one got underway and there were no notes of the stewards' final deliberations. The jockeys were exonerated on the grounds that they should have been given an opportunity to put their case again to the stewards and the stipendiaries were rightly disciplined because they should have ensured that they had a chance to do so. Poor Charles never headed a panel again. He should have been firmer with the stipendiaries. Would Victor or I have been? We will never know!

I had one other memorable moment at Haydock when I was in the chair and arrived to be told that a charity match which was to be televised between Sir Hugh Fraser and Clement Freud could not take place at the advertised time because Sir Hugh's plane had gone to Manchester airport and he was going to be late. When he finally arrived the match took place which set back the rest of the programme and sadly for Sir Hugh, Clement Freud won the contest convincingly. We held an enquiry and I had rung up to find the cloud ceiling at Haydock which was 900 feet. Having landed there several times in chartered planes myself I knew that the ceiling was above that which any competent professional pilot could land safely. Sir Hugh obviously expected his explanation to be accepted and when I pointed this out to him he got quite angry. His anger increased when I fined him £100 and he strode out of the room glaring at me in the process. The rumour spread the next day that he had bought Logan Airlines so that he could sack the pilot involved but whether there was any truth in that I didn't find out. There was a sequel though, because a few years later I found myself in a sauna at my favourite health farm, Grayshott Hall, with Clement Freud who told me that the high spot of his riding career had been his victory over Hugh Fraser. He had no idea that I had been senior steward and was very amused when I told him I had fined his opponent. The lengthy discussion caused us both to stay longer than we should have done in the sauna and the sight of the two of us emerging from it with, in my case, sweat literally pouring off me, cannot have been the most attractive sight other males in the changing room saw that day.

Fortunately when I became chairman of Bangor and then Chester my stewarding days on those two courses came to an end – chairmen of courses could not remain as stewards. I did however have a spell at Aintree and once a year I used to do a Friday evening and Saturday at Newmarket at two minor days mid-summer as the Jockey Club insisted that only their members should be in the chair. Aintree when I joined had Philip Leverhulme and John Derby both as active stewards. There was a head-on box with a rickety ladder which both those worthies and others on the panel refused to climb up and George Owen and myself found ourselves as the only two regularly sent out to it.

I quite enjoyed the Newmarket weekend although I felt sorry for the local stewards who struck me as being quite competent and I was pleased when the Jockey Club allowed them to take the chair a few years after I was committed to my weekend there. I had one interesting enquiry into an amateur race in which Julie Cecil and Willy Bissell got into a major barging match in the last two furlongs and Eve Johnson Houghton took advantage of their inability to keep their horses straight and came late to win the race. An enquiry was inevitable and the stipendiary came up to me and said, 'If they were professionals they would both get a week's suspension, but if you can deliver a really major rocket to both of them I will go with that.' Tommy Pilkington had said to me, 'I don't envy you this one,' as we went into the room and we duly played the film which showed, as I expected, both amateurs equally at fault. Julie Cecil took over the dialogue not allowing Bissell to get a word in and smiling sweetly she said, 'We didn't really do each other any damage did we, Willy?' I started to say that it was a quite disgraceful piece of riding from both of you when I caught sight of Julie's face which was red with anger and for a moment I thought she was coming across the table to attack me. I cut the rocket short and hastily finished the enquiry and when I returned to Jeremy Hindley, who I was staying with, he was convulsed with laughter and said, 'I have just had Julie

Cecil on the phone at length and suggest you have a large drink as she has a pack of Alsatians she would like to set on you.' Needless to say Julie and I later became the best of friends and had a good laugh over the whole incident.

During my many years of stewarding the Jockey Club started seminars for stewards which were an excellent idea although at the beginning old hands like me thought they were a waste of time. However, apart from educating stewards one of the main purposes was to get uniformity of decisions which was certainly a worthwhile aim. The one I remember best was in fact at Haydock. We had an uneventful morning and were allowed a couple of glasses of extremely mediocre wine at lunch which did at least relax us. After lunch the senior stipendiary announced he was having a session on non triers and started a film on the first one which showed a well known northern jockey going up and down and not doing a 'tap' and just as I was half asleep he said, 'Now I think you will find the second more interesting' – and I came totally awake when I realised the horse belonged to a friend of mine who I had encouraged to own horses and was trained by John Edwards, then my National Hunt trainer. The meeting was the first Cheltenham of the season and for some unknown reason my friend wanted his horse to have an easy race. John Edwards was on holiday in Spain but his more than competent assistant, Venetia Williams, was in charge and could have ensured that sensible instructions were give to Tom Morgan the stable jockey. Unfortunately Venetia, who was to become one of the most successful National Hunt trainers in the country, had a bad fall in an early race and my friend was left on his own to give Tom Morgan his orders for the race. At the seminar the film was played to about half way when the stipendiary stopped it and said, 'Morgan has the horse nicely buried, why on earth does he suddenly let the horse come out and see daylight?' At this point I completely forgot myself and said, 'The owner has spent the winter wondering just that.' Fortunately two friends shut me up immediately and the rest of the film was played showing an increasingly desperate Morgan again trying to bury the horse, finally finishing a close second. An enquiry was inevitable but with no stable representative to interview, the local stewards had to concentrate on Tom Morgan who apparently lapsed into 'broad Irish', and they eventually gave up and recorded his explanation. Very lucky for all concerned. The inevitable happened and my friend had a large bet next time, when the horse was comprehensively beaten.

The Jockey Club started to increase the number of days stewards had to act and as I got closer to the magic age of seventy when all stewards retire they increased the number of days from twelve to sixteen. This was too much for me as the only course I was acting on was Haydock and that was on the flat only. My last day of stewarding came and the course made a presentation at which Philip Arkwright, who always called a spade a spade, said, 'I thought they would have done better for you than that.' I went home and solemnly drank most of a bottle of Dom Pérignon I had been saving for a big occasion and there was nothing bigger than finishing stewarding. Sadly I had become rather disillusioned with the routine and boredom which accompanies most days stewarding. Having said that I have nothing but admiration for the numerous stewards, male and female, who do it just as competently and professionally as the stipendiaries who do it for a living. I am just simply amazed they enjoy it so much but at least they no longer have the media baying for professional stewards. The one thing that does sadden me is that the edict has now gone out that stewards should not drink at lunchtime. We had an unofficial golden rule, maximum of two glasses at lunch, but not a drink afterwards. Stewards were not helped by a trainer at Ludlow recently whose horse was disqualified and complaining to the stipendiary he said that the stewards at Ludlow were the same as ever, full of drink and incompetent – both utterly untrue and not intended to be taken seriously.

Anyway any steward seen drinking at lunchtime had to be reported to the stipendiary. Quite unnecessary and really racing should not take itself so seriously. Stewards are more than capable of knowing they must make sure that their judgement is not impaired. What would John Derby have thought of the edict? He used to come from a lunch at Knowsley and always have a glass of port at Haydock where a bottle was kept especially for him and not touched by the other stewards. Mind you, as he was one of the most difficult stewards I have ever stewarded alongside I have probably not picked the best example. I also do not like the current rules on interference, which have led Stewards to stop disqualifying winners. It seems to me that they are terrified of disqualifying a winner although they happily severely penalize the jockeys.

Chapter 11

Racecourse Management

I started off at Bangor-on-Dee, which was probably an ideal course to start as Bangor had plenty of problems when I joined the board. There were a number of local worthies headed by Philip Leverhulme and Lord Kenyon (whose obituary was my first for the *Daily Telegraph)*, was another. John Barlow was a third, Ririd Myddleton, the owner of Chirk Castle, another and Chubb Paterson, whose son, Owen, was recently in the Cabinet, yet another.

The course was unprofitable and all the early talk at board meetings was about survival. I did find it surprising that with all the wealth of board members this should be so but, felt very privileged to be amongst so many important people, I kept my head down at the early meetings. I always got on particularly well with Philip Leverhulme but unfortunately Chester was always his main priority and I felt his heart was never really into heading the Bangor board. He did bring in the Haydock management at one point but, similarly to my bringing in the Aintree management to Chester later, it did not really work and merely added to the overheads a small course had to bear.

The course was actually owned by Sara Rosselli, who sadly died at an early age and her husband, Peter, became the senior trustee of her large estate. Much of the estate was farmed by a Mr Done whose family had owned an outstanding sprinter, Alfrey Don, trained by Billy Dutton when Pat Rohan was his assistant. Far from being a friend and supporter of Bangor, Mr Done hated us and we nicknamed him the 'farmer from hell'. To some extent Philip Leverhulme's local prestige and standing kept him in check, but when Philip gave up and was succeeded by Malise Nicolson we felt the full brunt of Done's antagonism.

Malise was an excellent chairman. He had a successful business career as the 'primo' in the Port of Liverpool company and actually came to our annual lunch at the Savoy when I was on my year as president of the Export Group for the Construction Industries. Malise was representing Shipping.

Under his chairmanship the fortunes of Bangor improved as he accelerated what was badly needed, the reconstruction of the old buildings – two being particularly relevant, the new weighing room and the Nicholson building with a smart new restaurant and an excellent bar. Both cost a lot of money and I admit I had my doubts whether the course could afford them. I could not have been more wrong.

Bangor is the only course I know which has no grandstand and in fact, as a quite steep embankment makes a wonderful vantage point to watch racing in good weather, there is no need for one. I am absolutely convinced that a stand would be a disaster at Bangor and that the charm of this rural racecourse is enhanced by not having one.

I should at this point say that in the early days of Malise's chairmanship shares had been issued of five hundred pounds each, two being the maximum any individual could claim. My first wife, Jane, and I both claimed our maximum and like everybody else we never expected to see our money back but felt it was going to a very worthy cause. Why nobody had thought of it before I can't imagine!

In the meantime we had to negotiate with 'the farmer from hell' and whilst Philip Leverhulme had kept him in check, Malise had the impossible task of trying to do so and it was probably the most difficult issue he had to deal with before the devastating illness that was to end his life took hold.

I joined Chester racecourse just after a fire, which was certainly caused by arson, took hold and destroyed the main stand. Chester had also had a terrible year in 1969 when all three days of the May meeting were abandoned due to torrential rain which caused the river Dee, tidal below the Grosvenor Bridge (Chester was once a thriving port), to overflow. Philip Leverhulme told a wonderful story of how Lord Sefton then the Chester chairman and he went to see Lord Wigg at the Levy Board following the 1969 abandonment. They were subjected to a major lecture about how they had been totally unprepared for a financial catastrophe and that with better foresight and decent planning of financial reserves they could have avoided it. When Wigg paused for breath Sefton replied, 'Wigg, you are talking about finance. I have been very fortunate to inherit an enormous estate and have never had to worry about finance at any stage of my life and I am not starting now!' Philip told me if the ground could have swallowed him up he would have been grateful and any chance of getting money from the Levy Board went straight out of the window.

The fire was actually the best thing that every happened to Chester as with the insurance money we were able to build a stand far better and really well designed by a local architect from the brewing family, Duncan Boddington.

I enjoyed serving under Philip enormously. He ran the course through a general manager who had risen through the ranks and thought the world of his boss. He was slightly feudal in outlook and the board reflected this, consisting of Lord Hugh Cholmondeley, a charming man totally disinterested in racing, Sir John Hanmer who had inherited the baronetcy from Edward Hanmer, a considerable force in racing and who had lectured me on betting when I became a director of Bangor, and Geoffrey Churton who was always sensible and stayed on the board until well into his eighties. We had three councillors, as Chester Council actually owned the course although we owned part of the stands. Philip handled the councillors with great skill and they, like the rest of us, generally admired him. At the annual general meeting virtually none of the Chester shareholders who attended dared ask any serious question although Keith Rae, a local worthy, two or three times asked if a dividend could be paid, only to be severely put down by Philip.

By 1993 it was obvious that both Chester and Bangor would need to have a new chairman. Bangor because Malise Nicholson was in the grip of the illness which was to end his life and Chester because Philip Leverhulme, crippled with arthritis and approaching seventy-five, was finding it increasingly difficult to get round the course.

I did not expect to get or particularly want the chairmanship of Bangor. I knew that John Barlow was favoured by Malise but with retirement from my family company scheduled for the following year, to succeed Philip at Chester would suit me very well. John Barlow and I had been friends since our preparatory school days and could discuss the situation without embarrassment and John volunteered to go and see Philip to try and get an idea of his views on a successor for Chester and he came back with the strong indication that it was me who he wished to succeed him.

The Bangor succession came first and to my surprise John Barlow announced he did not want to take it, the reason becoming obvious when he parted from his wife, Susan, and kept a low profile. I was duly elected chairman and when a little later Philip asked me to succeed him at Chester I found myself chairing two racecourses. In addition I had earlier agreed to join Peter Daresbury on the board of Aintree and became involved in Aintree's great revival. So my business life had changed from construction to racecourse management.

At Bangor we continued to have to negotiate with 'the farmer from hell'. The worst of his actions was preventing us from taking National Hunt summer fixtures which were becoming available. Under the terms of his agreement with the landlord we were rationed to the fixtures we already had and any further ones had to be on terms Done agreed to, but his demands were such that it was impossible to take them. In addition he had started to grow maize on the inside of the track and this grew so high that by late summer it was only when the big screens came into existence that spectators could see the racetrack beyond.

After about four years my general manager abruptly resigned and having interviewed several unsatisfactory candidates Michael Webster, who had been in that position at Sandown Park, let it be known he was interested. He lived in Hampshire but agreed to buy a house locally and move his family. Although he was unable to honour that part of the agreement he did start to improve the fortunes of Bangor and he did open my eyes to the difference a real professional could make when he took charge. This was to be of great benefit to me at Chester.

At Chester I had a general manager who had worshipped Philip Leverhulme and although my relationship was satisfactory it was never going to be more than that and I tried to strengthen the management by bringing in Charles Barnett from Aintree as a consultant. Just as Bangor had brought in Haydock some years before, it did not really work, but Charles did point out to me the solution. He told me to approach Richard Thomas at Haydock who was frustrated by Jockey Club controls and would welcome a freer hand. Richard needed little persuasion to switch courses and so began a great chairman/chief executive partnership, the best and most productive of my business career.

Although Richard was incredibly young to be at the sharp end of Britain's oldest and almost most profitable flat course we both shared the same ambition – to take it from nearly the most profitable to the most profitable flat course in the country. I had also a number of things in my favour. Philip Leverhulme had been an excellent chairman but had been brought up in an era when food and drink were not as important as they were to become. I was chairman and co-founder of a medium size wine company and anxious to sell a lot of wine. We set out to create a network of bars and eating outlets which racegoers could really enjoy. The long room in the members had always been over crowded and as the outside bars took shape the pressure on it decreased. My racing friend, David Marchwood, British Chairman of Moet and Chandon, had helped to create two champagne bars at York and Newbury. York was a great success, particularly as the management subsidised the champagne, but Newbury was in the wrong place and never really took off. Chester's first new champagne bar just beyond the weighing room was such a success that we had to ration at times the number of customers there. A further bar just beyond the far end of the paddock is my favourite. It has a lot of space and one year a jazz band played there attracting many customers.

As we successfully sold more and more champagne pressure came to increase the number of both top and cheap brands and to my astonishment some of champagne's most famous names were offering us major discounts. Sadly I struggled to get Haynes, Hanson and Clark champagne sold around the racecourse as their champagne, Pierre Vaudon, was made by a co-operative who had less problem selling their excellent produce (quite an amount went into top brands) than others. There was a good story about our first cheapie, Boizel, which we were able to offer well below the price of others, including Pierre Vaudon. We sold so much the first year that Madame Boizel decided to visit us and Richard was extremely nervous as to how I was going to behave towards her. She came to lunch in the directors' room and shortly came up to me, 'How are you enjoying your champagne, Monsieur?' 'I am enjoying it enormously, Madame, it is delicious,' I replied. She smiled sweetly and I did not tell her that I was drinking a glass of Pierre Vaudon from the next door box of Ces Jenkins. Richard who was watching the exchange immediately sent over a waitress with Boizel who suggested she filled up my glass. To nobody's surprise, I politely declined.

We also made major improvements to the course, including a network of drainage to try and prevent a disaster like 1969 when all three May days were lost. This did save us later when appalling weather threatened the May meeting. Although the meeting was saved the main car parks in the middle of the course were unusable and a decision had to be taken to let our customers find car parking elsewhere. This was a decision facing the directors in 1969 when racing would probably have been possible at least on the third day but the board then could not see how the car park problem could be resolved.

My chief role as chairman was to examine Richard's many ideas and try and get him to concentrate on those that I thought were viable. These included the take over of other racecourses and a number were looked at but the problem was that Northern Racing and Arena Leisure had taken over the obvious ones, and there were few independents that were suitable. We did look quite hard at Wetherby but I had two concerns – the distance from us and the amount of racing available to racegoers in the area. In the end we went back to the obvious candidate, the local course, Bangor-on-Dee. I was in a very difficult position as chairman of both and had to start the next Bangor board meeting with the words 'In my capacity as chairman of Chester I have to tell you that we would like to bring the two courses together'. I then left the meeting for half an hour while the rest of the Bangor board deliberated a response. I was sure Michael Webster had anticipated the situation and his own position had been weakened by advising me of an approach by a southern jumps course who he thought would offer him a contract, though unfortunately for him they did not finalise the offer.

I was determined to take no part in the negotiation over Bangor and Richard's first job was to persuade Peter Rosselli that the takeover was a good idea. Fortunately Peter was able to offer Mr Done another piece of land to farm and to hand over the inside of the track for us to farm and the negotiation went far better than Richard or I expected. We were undoubtedly helped by the fact that the shareholders who had stumped up their five hundreds when times were tough could now expect a hefty sum which they never expected. The Bangor negotiators extracted a full price and I asked Charles Lowther to take the chairmanship and he is still in that position today.

Richard then turned his attention to developing the land the other side of the railway near the seven furlong start. A big new stable block was constructed so that the horses no longer had to walk down a busy road before entering the paddock. Surprisingly trainers had objected to this far less than we would have expected. A local housing company joined us and a very successful housing development was completed. Part of the owners' and trainers' car park became a hotel under the Inter Continental franchise and the occupancy has risen steadily, despite increased competition, and stands at ninety-four per cent today.

I had fairly readily agreed to most of these moves but I was really nervous about the next one – the takeover of the course's catering. I have to say Richard was at his absolute best over this, employing a large local firm, Heathcotes, as a joint partner before taking over completely. There were two big advantages, the first that the food was upgraded and the second that we got all the profit on the alcohol which made more money than the food. The catering was extended to local interests including the town hall and Chester racecourse is now the largest local outside caterer in the area. A full time seven-days-a-week restaurant named the 1539 (the year racing at Chester started) was opened at the entrance to Tattersalls and recently a seven-days-a-week pub has opened in the centre of the course and does a thriving trade summer and winter.

The bravest move of all after my time as chairman was to refuse Fred Done's offer of Tote facilities and start a fixed betting operation, Chester Bets, which many said was doomed to failure. It is in fact extremely successful, although Richard Thomas admitted it would not suit all courses. It is strange that more large courses have not followed us.

Chester Racecourse Company is no longer a racecourse but a major leisure company with a considerable influence on the city and its surrounds. It is the leading flat racecourse which declares its profits yearly, though Ascot and York would probably be ahead if they operated on the same basis. Nevertheless Chester, the oldest racecourse in the country, is still right at the top after nearly five hundred years of racing.

I was asked by Peter Daresbury to join him on the board of Aintree after he became chairman nearly thirty years ago. Aintree had been saved miraculously from the developers which has been described elsewhere in the book, and Peter had the daunting task of bringing back a racecourse which had seen some dreadful management and which was targeted by the lunatic fringe of the animal rights brigade on its one great day of the year, Grand National day. He did however have some factors in his favour. Ivan Straker, the English chairman of Seagrams, was a great lover of Aintree and the National and he and Peter were to bring Patrick Martell, whose brandy company had been bought by Seagrams, more and more into the picture. The course was extremely run down and Peter and I had frequent discussions on the areas which needed most attention. He had appointed as managing director John Parrot who was doing an excellent job. Sadly, relatively early on in the story of the revival of Aintree he was to meet a tragic end hunting as Peter's guest with the Wynnstay Hunt. John is just one of a number of people I have known to die on the hunting field and hunting is probably one of the most dangerous sports in existence today.

Faced with the prospect of finding a chief executive at short notice we considered all the options and came up with the name of Charles Barnett, a great friend of Peter's and a good friend of mine. The partnership of Peter as chairman and Charles as chief executive was to see Aintree become a highly profitable and successful course again and to prove that a pair of competent people at the top is the right way to get the best out of running a racecourse.

I soon realised that Aintree was quite different to Cheltenham and other National Hunt tracks in that all its profit was earned on the three days of the National meeting. However hard we all tried, and we were under great pressure from the Jockey Club to expand the fixture list, we could not make the extra fixtures we received really profitable.

In the early days all the television revenues accrued to the course, which made a great difference to Aintree's finances. In recent years the revenues have been split around a number of Jockey Club courses which was not helpful to Aintree. National day gets by far the largest television audience of the year and it is a shame that the course does not derive greater financial benefit from it. A large television audience has disadvantages when much of the audience who watch racing only occasionally react unfavourably when horses are tragically killed.

The National brought in wrath from the public and reaction from the RSPCA – who had, for a short time, a chief executive who was controversial to put it mildly and who has now thankfully departed. One of the horses killed was the Gold Cup winner Synchronised. He was completely uninjured from the fall but galloping round the course he sustained a freak injury which could have happened on any National Hunt course in Britain or Ireland. The media nevertheless fed on the national frenzy and sensible racing correspondents were probably leant on by their editors whose main job is to sell large numbers of newspapers. As a result the board dramatically altered the fences and the stiff cores which existed in the years I was on the board were changed and the fences became much easier to jump – some of the famous ones like Becher's and the Canal Turn now being utterly different.

In the early days Peter and Charles really concentrated on those that mattered at the top of the BBC and a great deal of entertainment helped to cement the relationship. The weekend I remember most vividly was at Herez in Spain where the Aintree board, Patrick Martell and a number of BBC personnel, including Clare Balding and Des Lynham, all gathered together for golf and evening entertainment. I was partnered with Patrick Martell for one of the two days golf and was not at my best but the evening was very interesting. Sandemans were the hosts and we had to endure five different sherries with dinner which, as I don't really like sherry, caused me to imbibe much less than usual. I eagerly went for the excellent Bordeaux on offer with the steak only to find we were not getting a second glass. When it came to the brandy I reluctantly said no as I don't drink brandy, but Des Lynham next to me said, 'That brandy you have turned down is fifteen hundred dollars a glass in Hong Kong.' I hastily re-summoned the waiter and finished up drinking two beakers! After dinner the Flamenco dancers came on and after an excellent display they invited us all to join them. Peter, Charles and Des Lynham joined them enthusiastically but Clare and I found two pillars to hide behind before Des Lynham spotted both of us who were dragged onto the floor. My partner could not have been nicer and whispered, 'Just follow me.' I survived the ordeal; what happened to Clare I could not see.

The two major dramas in my time were the false start fiasco and the bomb hoax. I watched the false start from the 'roof' stand in the Princess Royal box and I turned to a man next to me I had never seen before and said, 'The starter is losing all control, he is never going to start this race' – unduly prophetic as it turned out. One false start having taken place he then shouted out 'False start' a second time but the 'flag man' down the course, paid a pittance, failed to hear him and to our horror the jockeys continued – although it was obvious to the spectators that a race was not taking place. Nobody emerged with a great deal of credit though in my opinion the starter was almost entirely to blame. He came from a military background and was very pedantic in his attitude to jockeys. We all wanted Gerry Scott to start the race, but the Jockey Club insisted on the senior man taking charge. Fortunately they were to change their minds the following year and things have greatly improved since then. I do think the current way of starting National Hunt races is admirable and wonder why it wasn't thought of earlier.

Aintree had always, with its Irish connections, been a likely target for the IRA and Charles Barnett took the threat seriously – we had instructions and personal radios in the event of a major problem. In 1997 the three-day meeting was going particularly well and Angela and I were entertaining the winners of the Aintree hurdle, the race then before the National, when the dreaded signal went and I left Angela and rushed to Charles Barnett's office. I will never forget the expression on Charles's face as he gave us the news that the police wanted us to evacuate the course. He knew, as we all did, that racing was over for the day and we all had to leave the building and head for the temporary hut the police used near what is now the National start. Peter and Charles soon managed to make out that they were too important to be left there and extracted themselves but Richard Fildes and I were the two directors left there as was Peter O'Sullivan who also ended up in the building. After an hour the heating broke down and the building got very cold. I have never received the credit due for persuading the most senior policeman there that he had to get Peter O'Sullivan out too as Peter was beginning to look very grey and of course none of us had the ideal clothing for a cold April evening. Richard and I were to remain there for a few hours and I made strenuous attempts to get my mobile to work. There must have been thousands of others trying the same thing and it was probably a couple of hours later when I got through to Nicky Henderson's office. Until recently Nicky always stayed with me for the National meeting and his secretary was still in the office when I rang. 'Don't worry about anyone,' she said cheerfully, 'they have all found a wonderful pub and are having a great time.'

Richard and I were eventually (around ten o'clock) taken to the same pub which had made a fortune by charging entry fees to get a drink. Fortunately the whisky had not run out and we both had two large ones before embarking on the search for a taxi. It turned out that our driver had been driving around Liverpool for years but had never embarked on a journey as far afield as Tilstone Fearnall near Tarporley. When he got to the gates of my drive he stopped the car and said in amazement, 'What on earth are those?' He had actually never seen rabbits running around in the wild before!

A decision was taken to run the race on Monday and Peter Daresbury asked me if I wanted to look after the Princess Royal or accompany and do a commentary for John and Norma Major, who were in the last days of an election campaign. As the Majors had been to our house at Tilstone for a Conservative function and as I had been to Downing Street several times in his spell as Prime Minister, I thought I should accompany them. In the end I was to regret my decision. We fought through the crowd to get the Majors to the box they were to watch from. John Major showed no interest in the proceedings and declined my offer of a commentary. We had real difficulty getting him to his car after the race because a fiercely hostile crowd booed and jostled them. Worst of all Stan Clark won the race and I missed all the celebration in the winner's enclosure. Charles Barnett had done a fantastic job to get the race restaged. His decision not to touch the main car park until after the race and his security arrangements meant he could be certain the course was secure and despite several hoax calls he never considered calling the race off. The searches were very thorough and to this day the Aintree National three days remain a meeting where rigorous searches still take place.

My last major duty at Aintree was to keep an eye on the large development to build a new stand, paddock and weighing-room complex on behalf of the board. I was sorry to lose the old paddock which I felt had much more character than the new, but the stand was a great success. My one moment of panic was when I realised at Ascot that the sight lines for their new stand were all wrong and I rang up the site manager for the Aintree stand and fixed a meeting for the following Monday. Fortunately there was no problem and the whole development was a great success.

Peter had gained me a few years over the normal Jockey Club retirement age of seventy. Leaving the Aintree board also meant the end of active participation in racecourse matters although the Chester board were kind enough to make me president which at least left a link with my favourite racecourse. They also give me a picture of the course and members stand with Richard and I together in the paddock on race day. I hope one day it will hang in the directors' room!

Chapter 12

My Trainers

I have, I suppose, had quite a number of trainers under both rules. This is not because I have fallen out with many of them, it just seems to have happened that way. I list them in roughly chronological order.

Rosemary Lomax was my first trainer and I remember her with tremendous affection. She had a very difficult time with her husband Ian having to hold the licence until the Jockey Club allowed ladies to be licenced. She was always short of owners and spent much of her time trying to acquire them and she literally wore herself out trying to talk some very moderate people into horse ownership. Her triumph with Precipice Wood in 1970 was the first time a female trainer had won a major Group One race. Whilst brilliant with horses, she was less assertive with jockeys and stable staff and Ian had to step in and help her on that front. She was forced to retire far too early and rang me up several times to say she wanted to write a book and I offered to help but it never materialised.

Doug Francis, my second trainer, was a wonderful man and became a very great friend. Although his younger brother, Dick, was far more famous, Doug enjoyed a happy and successful career. His owners were a varied bunch, from Anne, Duchess of Westminster to the chairman of the Levy Board, Lord Wigg. Doug was not the best communicator on how the horses were progressing and on one memorable occasion, a long-time owner rang to ask how his horse was, to be told it had won at Stratford that very afternoon.

If Doug had a fault it was that he was too lenient on his horses, as his daughter Susan was always telling him. I often wonder what would have resulted if Ginger Nut, who finished a close up fifth in the Grand National, had had one more serious gallop. He did train one very good horse, Roughlyn, and I have told the story elsewhere of Lester's efforts to get aboard him.

My best man at my second wedding, Doug went in with Angela when the bride and bridegroom were called out and for a brief moment was taken as the bridegroom by the Registrar. He was present at both my major triumphs with Cormorant Wood and his driving us back from Manchester airport to our house at Swettenham was almost as hairy as the Champion Stakes itself.

I gave the address at his funeral, the only time I have taken several 'rescue' pills to get through it. If I had known Dick Francis was recording it, I don't think I would have ever made it. I went to see him three days before he passed away; he was as cheerful as ever and when I said I would come again the following Saturday, he said, 'Don't bother because I won't be here; I have had a great life so don't worry about me.' He said much the same thing to his brother, Dick, who always sent him a copy of his latest book. Although more literary than Dick he always said he never read a line of them. The first editions must be worth a lot of money now.

Pat Rohan, who had married Jack Bissell's niece, Mary, was my third trainer. A very nice man he was extremely highly strung and if he had not been a strict teetotaller, I would have wondered whether a drink would have calmed him down. We had a couple of good horses, Stynog Wood and Oswestry Covert, and also the dam of Cormorant Wood, Quarry Wood. Stynog Wood started off at 5/2 on in a flat race at the Aintree National meeting but got left at the start. She made amends at Ayr and followed up by winning the Lily Agnes at Chester's May festival. She should, in my view, have then been second to Waterloo, who won the Queen Mary at Royal Ascot but her jockey got her shut in and she finished fourth.

Quarry Wood finished fifth in the Chester Cup with an apprentice, claiming seven on her. The boy looked delighted until I asked him whether he realised there was now a prize for fourth place (it had just been introduced) and the smile quickly disappeared. The race had its consequences, because she ran so well in a long distance race both Barry Hills and I were convinced that Cormorant Wood would stay a mile and a half.

Pat was a keen bridge player and we had some memorable games, including one at his home in Malton, when he got Mrs Duncan Davidson and Mrs Brotherton, the original owner of Red Rum, to make up the four. We also had a weekend in Ireland, where he arranged golf for me, while he and Jane went hunting. Jane enjoyed it but Pat had a bad fall and failed to make the party in the evening.

Barry Hills was my main flat trainer and became a very good friend. We had over twenty holidays together and I can never remember us having a serious argument. His Lambourn stables were on quite a slope and you knew where you were in the pecking order when you came to see your horse. If he was in one of the small 'out' yards away from the main yard, prospects were definitely not good. The horses also had to go some way to the gallops down a busy main road but all that changed when Barry moved first to Manton and then, when Robert Sangster put Manton on the market, to a new stable complex about a mile away from the old. Although Barry was upset leaving Manton he handled the negotiation with the council very cleverly by threatening to close down the stable unless he got planning permission for housing on his old site and permission for the new complex. The housing permission financed all the new building. He had originally started training in 1969, having had a massive win in the Lincoln when he was head lad to John Oxley. The win financed his start up as a trainer and I well remember his horses just appearing on the gallops at Lambourn. Rosemary Lomax said, 'Those belong to a new trainer called Hills, I wonder how long he will be with us?' Success came quite early with Rheingold, narrowly beaten in the Derby but then winning the Prix de L'Arc de Triomphe. Robert had a number of horses with him and I remember the two of us having lunched rather too well before the first race at Goodwood where he had the favourite and, suddenly remembering the race was about to take place, he sprinted out of the restaurant, through two enclosures and got to the bookmakers just in time to put a major bet on, followed by me with a much smaller one. Peter Marsh who had lunch with us tried to follow us and not being very fit struggled to keep up and complained bitterly that the price had contracted sharply by the time he got there. He also was sadly to die a couple of months later. Ernie Johnson who was having his first ride for Robert asked Barry where the owner had got to. 'Don't worry about him, he's doing the important work,' replied Barry. The horse duly won and the celebrations started.

As Barry's success increased, his need for a top-class jockey grew and Robert solved that problem by bringing over Steve Cauthen from America. Steve had phenomenal success in the States, riding his first winner at 16, he had ridden the Triple Crown winners in America and 487 winners in a season. Cormorant Wood was the only top-class horse I had with Barry but she was right at the top of the tree being listed by Steve Cauthen as one of the top seven horses he had ever ridden in the Turf Directory 1993 at the end of his career.

She was not fashionably bred, by Home Guard out of Quarry Wood who had won two small races and should have been fourth in the Chester Cup as explained above. Home Guard's best distance was seven furlongs to a mile. Undoubtedly Home Guard had a major influence on Cormorant Wood's stamina. For the whole of her season as a three-year-old both Barry and I were convinced she would stay at least a mile and a half. In fact she stayed no further than a mile and a quarter.

Both Barry and I had started to enjoy holidays in Barbados and he had rented a house called Woodlands at the Speightstown end of Cobbler's Beach. The house could be divided in two and Angela and I decided to join him and take half the house. This worked very well and we had several tremendous holidays there. Barry's popularity with numerous jockeys and trainers ensured a constant stream of visitors calling in for drinks at all hours of the day. Two of his guests were Nick and Diana Henderson. Nicky was terribly restless and used to pace the beach in the early hours. How do I know? Because I used to go to the loo in the early hours and saw him out of the window.

We all decided we wanted a change and settled on Cape Town where, on a friend of mine, William Midwood's 'recommendation' we rented a nice house in Constantia from Ian Overstone. Dick Bonnycastle, one of Barry's main owners and a prominent Canadian businessman, joined us and we had eight or nine excellent holidays there. One of the problems was a shortage of good bedrooms. The master bedroom which Angela and I had was fine, and Dick's was improved by Ian but Barry and Penny's, separate from us, was definitely inferior. The second problem was safety. Ian's back drive was 'open to the four winds' which was very unusual in South Africa where large amounts were spent on making houses as safe as possible. As crime increased in Cape Town we became increasingly nervous and a terrible murder in a Cape stall half a mile down the road was the last straw. The lady running it came in early on a Sunday to open up and was confronted by thieves who forced her to open the till and when they had taken the cash they filled a nearby pail with water and drowned the poor lady in it. Life is very cheap in South Africa.

I have to say that on the one occasion Ian's maid saw an intruder about eleven o'clock at night, security were there in two minutes from her call and the police in four – very impressive. Sadly that was the end of our holidays together. We played a lot of golf which was fought out by the three of us in a fiercely competitive spirit and there were some memorable incidents; one I will never forget was when Barry sent his young caddy into a wood after a wild shot off the first at the Clovelly Golf Club. The caddy came out and said there is a large snake over your ball. 'What do I do now?' said Barry. I replied, 'You play with another ball; it is a two stroke penalty or you can play it where it lies'

– a slight sense of humour failure! We also hired an excellent cook and drank gallons of South African wine particularly the local white, Klein Constantia, which was delicious although when I tried to drink it in England it simply didn't taste the same. Angela and I stayed in South Africa for a few years at Cape Town's premier hotel, the Mount Nelson, which I liked very much. It had a wonderful swimming pool and sunbathing area. My cousin Bill McAlpine stayed there also in one of the private suites with its own pool. We always had two dinners with each of us paying in turn. Despite four courses and the best South African wine we could never get the bill over twenty pounds a head in English money.

Barry decided to try Mauritius largely because Penny, wisely, wanted to cut down on the alcohol and although he spent an extra day there because of a minor hurricane he has gone back every year since. Angela and I had one holiday with them but found the island incredibly expensive and the two hotels we were in had poor sea bathing. This did not bother Barry who does not swim and when I went to pay my bill on the final morning I found myself alongside Raymond Mould who said, 'I have fourteen racehorses and share a yacht; they seem quite cheap compared to a holiday here!' Barry continued to train a large number of winners. He won the 2000 Guineas in 2004 and the 1000 five years later, but the Derby eluded him. His major illness with throat cancer and a number of complications went on for nearly five months and Penny never left his side, booking a room at the Stafford hotel and not seeing her home for the first three weeks. When I went to visit Barry in hospital towards the end of his very lengthy stay there, he told me in typical fashion, 'They all thought I was going to die, but I didn't!' When he came out he couldn't talk and had a pad to write on. One of his first visitors was his farrier who had sent him cards and a book. Expecting some thanks he waited for Barry to write on the pad and got exactly five words, 'you're still too f*****g expensive'.

Penny persuaded him to hand over the licence to Charles, who has been very successful to date. Retirement never suited Barry, who continued to take a major interest in the stable. Sheikh Hamdam offered him thirty horses to train which had previously been with another trainer and the use of his own gallops near Lambourn. Barry put the horses in his elder son John's name but after John's tragic early death they went back into Barry's name and he is now a fully licenced trainer again and his wonderful career is scheduled to finally finish at the end of the 2015 season.

Robert Sangster also introduced me to trainer **Jeremy Hindley**, who he had a few horses with. I have described my time with Jeremy as a trainer in the chapter, Middle Age. It was when Jeremy realised he was definitely an alcoholic that he decided to cease training and seek a cure. He went for a lengthy period of treatment to his old family home near Gisburn, Yorkshire, which had become a private nursing home and emerged a different and, in my view, a much nicer man. When Barry Hills and I met him again he confronted us with the words, 'You two both drink too much but you are not alcoholics, I am!'

Shortly afterwards he decided to move to South Africa where he set up in a half-way house in Cape Town for recovering alcoholics to spend a short period before entering the real world again. He had a full and happy life in South Africa with his second wife Vanessa, which was badly interrupted when he was diagnosed with Motor Neurone disease. He went to the Mayo Clinic in the hope they would give him an extended period of life but they only gave him five years. In typical fashion he set out to prove them wrong and lived a great deal longer. He fought the disease with great courage and continued to lead an active life although his body slowly began to deteriorate. My obituary to him was the last I wrote for the *Daily Telegraph* and because I knew him so well it only took me a couple of hours to write.

Nicky Henderson was my first National Hunt trainer and we got off to a wonderful start with River Ceiriog who won the Supreme Novice at the Cheltenham festival at the amazing odds of forty to one and was also about the easiest winner I have ever had, being in total command from half way down the back straight. Earlier in the day I had been to a Hall Engineering board meeting as I was for many years a non-executive director. Being driven from Stafford to Cheltenham I had a formbook and went through the race and decided it wasn't the strongest renewal. When I got to Cheltenham, where Nicky and I, our two wives and others were having lunch together, I said that I thought I should have an each way bet. Save your money and put it on Baby Sigh (another horse I had with Nicky) he is a certainty at Wolverhampton on Friday said Nicky. Baby Sigh got beaten at five to two on, but I did have a small each way bet on River Ceirog. The race was sponsored by Waterford Glass and I received sixty nine pieces of it, much of it wine glasses which are with me today. Nicky also got some wonderful glass and when I go to lunch or dinners at Seven Barrows the glass sits proudly on his table as it does on mine. Nicky is in fact the worst tipster I have ever come across. He has stayed with me every year up to the last two years for the Aintree festival but sadly Angela has now decided she is not well enough to cope with a large house party.

Nicky's horses are always finely tuned for Cheltenham where he is usually very successful and Aintree three weeks later is not always in the same category. In fact he had a period of fifty-nine successive losers at Aintree – a very expensive period for me as Nicky fancied a lot of them. The worst meeting was when he said after arriving, whatever happens I am sure to win the last race of the meeting, I have an outstanding bumper horse who is not fully exposed. I had my double maximum on and Nicky's other horse in the race won unbacked at fifty-to-one! Another major disaster was when he came to stay the night before a Bangor-on-Dee meeting, where he told me he did not fancy his principal owner's (the Queen Mother) horse the next day. These results are both recounted in my Betting chapter.

In fact trainers with large numbers of horses make life very difficult for their owners to spend a lot of time on the form book. Barry Hills did once employ Mathew Tester the Jockey Club leading handicapper and Mathew told me what a difficult time he had if his conclusions didn't accord with Barry's wishes. I only used one training establishment, the Ramsden's, which gave an accurate and unbiased assessment of a horse's chances. Most trainers like to be optimistic. Jack Ramsden was, if anything, basically a pessimist.

Nicky and I have remained great friends although I haven't had a horse with him for a few years. Like many of us he has been through a difficult marriage break-up but happily he and Diana have readjusted and both are now their old selves. Sophie, Nicky's partner, has not had an easy time either and has handled matters extremely well.

Anthony Johnson has been a friend for much of my life and was for a brief period a trainer, when he trained a couple of horses for me in his Upper Lambourn yard. One American bred did win a race.

I am not sure whether **John Edwards** or **Gordon Richards** was chronologically my second National Hunt trainer but whereas both had had a lot of ability and both had serious marriage break-ups, I have far more to say about John, who has been a close friend for many years. A colourful character always known as 'Jockey' he was presumably a capable amateur though his riding days were behind him when I got to know him. I suppose one of the reasons for my joining him was due to my sister's good horse Pearlyman who was trained by John for my sister Valerie and Willie Jenks, who shared him jointly. The horse won the Queen Mother champion two mile chase twice and according to Peter Scudamore, who rode him in the first, he was just about the best horse he had ever ridden. Not easy to train because of leg trouble, John deserves a lot of credit for his handling of Pearlyman.

He had quite a bit of land in a most attractive part of Herefordshire with the River Wye in the middle. A very fine fisherman, he once tried to give me a casting lesson with a fly rod but after two disasters with casting into trees on the opposite bank we gave up and on a very hot day went to the nearest pub. He did take me twice to the Devonshire beat on the River Blackwater where I spun for the fish, catching fifteen the first year in three days and eight large fish in two days the following year. There was an amazing Gillie known as Paddy who looked after us all and took a particular interest in me because I had several horses – he was an insatiable punter. On the last morning, having caught two big fish, I hooked another and started running down stream as the fish took off. 'Run faster sir or you'll lose the fish,' 'If I run any faster Paddy I'll have a heart attack,' 'Better that than lose the fish.' I still lost the fish. Lunch was in an old cricket pavilion and incredibly hot and totally exhausted I drank a bottle and a half of white wine and after lunch I said, 'Forget about me' – and lay down on the bare floor and went to sleep for two hours.

John's marital life was exciting to say the least and his devoted wife Gina had a difficult time. My own wife Angela had met Jockey before me and had gone racing with her cousin Antony Perry finishing up at Jockey's house where she spent the night. Although a great deal of drink had been consumed she had the good sense to lock the main door of her bedroom and the side door leading to the bathroom. Sure enough she was just getting to sleep when there was a rattle on the main door followed by an even quieter rattle on the side door half a minute later. 'Comes to something when I can't get into a room in my own house,' said John the next morning. John had a very pleasant shoot, the only problem being that there were not really enough drives for a full day. He solved this by making every excuse to start as late as possible and by having a long alcoholic lunch. The afternoon drive was his best. The problem being you had to have the right draw to get a lot of shooting. The first time I shot there John realised that I (then an attractive owner prospect) had a bad draw after lunch. He tried to put in a short extra drive at the end of the morning to drive a small coppice. Only one other gun accompanied us, the others all going back to the house. I suggested to John that Steve Cauthen would enjoy the shoot and he issued an invitation, telling me he had organised an attractive employee as Steve's date. It took me less than ten minutes after Annabel had been introduced to Steve to realise that she only had eyes for one person in the house and that was not Steve, but her employer, and she became his principal girlfriend when John and Gina parted. Her father had business dealings with John Hall and I met him at Charnes a couple of times. He quizzed me about his daughter's relationship with John and ended by saying, 'Tell him if he treats my daughter badly I will come and shoot him and I never miss.' Two years later John and I were together shooting grouse at Swinton, where I had persuaded Tim Kitson to bring John in to his team there. We had paused between drives at the edge of the main road from Lofthouse when I saw a Range Rover approaching and said I think this is Annabel's father, Mr Curragh Briggs, and sure enough he was driving with Annabel's brother in the passenger seat. John's relationship with Annabel was virtually over and he went very pale and half hid behind me. I could see a very ugly scene developing as the Range Rover slowed down and the driver had a very good look at us. To my intense relief he decided not to stop but it was a nasty moment.

While I never had a top-class horse with John I had a number of useful ones, Star of Screen and Cliffalda probably being the two best. Star of Screen won the Eider Chase and Cliffalda was good enough to run in the Aintree hurdle and was ridden by Tom Morgan who was due to ride the favourite Dixon House in the next race, the Grand National. I waited outside the weighing room but he charged past me heading for the loo and although I waited for over ten minutes, showed no signs of coming out. Dixon House fell early in the National! Other useful animals were Gerami, half owned by Robert Stangster's godson, and Deep Flash in partnership with Sir Eric Parker. He won first time out but didn't quite hit the heights we hoped for.

John had a very good track record. He won two Champion two mile chases and came within a whisker of winning a Gold Cup at Cheltenham. He had trained a winner of the Grand National until a few months before the race yet his stable was to disintegrate in the space of a single National Hunt season and incredibly John appeared to make little effort to stop his horses going to two main beneficiaries, Kim Bailey and Nigel Twiston Davies. Whilst Gina had undoubtedly contributed a great deal to the establishment and had particularly worked on the owner-trainer relationships he had a very competent assistant in Venetia Williams and an excellent staff. To this day I never understood why he didn't make more effort with the owners instead of blaming them for a lack of loyalty. For whatever reason he gave up and went to live in Ireland with his partner Avena Maxwell, now his second devoted wife, and he successfully buys horses there, particularly for Nicky Henderson. He is an excellent judge of a horse and has steadily made many successful purchases.

Gordon Richards attracted my attention because I was told how cheap he was compared to Newmarket and Lambourn trainers and when I had a horse with him I found that was indeed the case. I once asked him why he was so much cheaper and he replied, 'Bobby, I lead a very enjoyable life and make quite enough for my needs.' He was married for the second time to Joanie, a very smart, attractive lady, who was a cousin of a local landowner at Greystoke near Penrith, where Gordon trained. Unfortunately Joanie decamped with the same cousin and Gordon's life went downhill as a result. He had one outstanding horse in my last days with him, One Man, who had a fatal fall at Aintree over the Mildmay fences. Gordon was not a well man by this time and having had an outstanding career I am sure the double blow of Joanie's departure and One Man's demise did nothing to improve his health. I went to his funeral at Greystoke, one of the best attended I have ever been to, and I will always remember my many visits to the place in happier days which I enjoyed so much. His son took over the stables and has been successful.

Fred Rimell was a very close friend of Doug Francis, who was by now acting more as my racing adviser than my trainer. I had a number of horses with him of which Zip Fastener was easily the most memorable. Fred and his wife Mercy first came in to my life when Jeremy Vaughan sent horses there, culminating in Nicholas Silver's great win in the Grand National. In a way the win was fortunate; Nicholas Silver had to have fast ground and in those days, with no watering, it was possible to get it and the going was very fast; if my memory is correct, described as Good to Firm. There would be no chance of a horse getting that ground in a National nowadays; safety concerns ensure that the word 'Firm' will never appear in the going report. An excellent watering system ensures that the course can now control the going to a large degree. Jeremy had won a preparatory race for the National at the Cheltenham Festival, the Kim Muir, a well-known amateur Bill Tellwright was on board and a tremendous celebration followed.

Fred was a top-class trainer and engaged the Champion Jockey, Terry Biddlecombe. Brian Jenks had gone to Fred and ploughed money into his stable, becoming the leading National Hunt owner of his day. I would love to say that Brian was devoted to the sport but am afraid his main ambition was to get elected to the Jockey Club and once he had achieved that objective his participation waned somewhat, although he continued to own a reduced number of horses. I was never a big owner of Fred's but for some time had two or three horses with him. Zip Fastener gave me a lot of excitement. He won the Victor Ludorum hurdle at Haydock beating Fred's other runner, whose owner was furious. Fred had to rush over to him to try and pacify him and

Mercy accompanied us to the winners enclosure where Christine Sangster presented the trophy. In those days the Victor Ludorum was the main trial for the four-year-old hurdle at Cheltenham, the Triumph, and I fancied him quite strongly but Jeff King who had ridden him at Haydock, got him off last of twenty-three runners and he never got into the race. He became a more than useful chaser and won a number of races including one at Uttoxeter ridden by Terry Biddlecombe. Unfortunately the jockeys changing room was quite separate from the weighing room and Terry momentarily went there just before realising he hadn't weighed in. He hastened to correct the error but too many people had seen what had happened and the stewards had to have an enquiry. Philip Leverhulme was the senior steward and accepted the error was unintentional and the horse was weighed in and backers received their winnings. However a subsequent Jockey Club enquiry reversed the decision and the race was taken from us. The owner who had the eventual winner complained furiously to the *Racing Post* (or *Sporting Life* which was going then) that he had not been paid for his wagers on his horse. A subsequent letter to the paper pointed out that he was the luckiest man alive, to receive the winner's prize money despite being well beaten in the race and the one person who had a right to complain was Bobby McAlpine, who had lost his prize money through no fault of his own horse!

Zip Fastener, still with Fred, came to a sad end at Haydock when he finished third but put his foot in a divot just before the finishing line and pulled up with a broken leg just after the post and had to be put down. Fred insisted Mercy took me to the bar and dealt with the drama himself, sparing me the ordeal of watching the end of a much loved horse!

I also had a filly with the Rimells, called Precipienne She won a race but disappointed afterwards and the Rimells did not think she was genuine. As a result I sold her for a few hundred pounds. Precipienne was later sold for 60,000 guineas and the dam was to breed Preciptack still in my ownership and about the best stayer in South Africa, and then Forgive and Forget, who won one Cheltenham Gold Cup and would have won another if he hadn't had a fatal fall. Racing does have its ups and downs!

The horse that finished my association with the Rimells was my good hunter-chaser Compton Lad who I originally sent to them. He came back for a summer's rest to my stud at Emral which I shared with the Broad family, great friends of Doug Francis, who happened to be there. He was bleeding from a cut to his leg which the box driver said he had before being loaded. When Doug rang Fred to complain he got an earful from Fred who told him he had got the wrong horse despite the fact that Compton Lad was a grey. I would probably have sent the horse back to the Rimells had the Broads not insisted the horse went to...

Michael Dickenson who they had become friendly with. There was a subsequent drama when the next year I was at a Midland's racecourse with my sister Valerie and her husband, Peter Shaw. We were having lunch and Peter said, 'Don't look now but behind you is a lady dressed in black glaring furiously at you.' The lady turned out to be Mercy and when I sought out Fred he said, 'Bobby, you and I will never fall out but I can't talk for the missus.' I was very thrilled when Mercy, now in her nineties, had a runner in the Grand National a few years ago and sent her daughter Scarlett over who said, 'Mother would like you to go into the paddock with her.' I was touched!

Michael Dickenson took over one of the best prospective hunter-chasers in the country and he was a genuine hunter-chaser. Readers may not realise that many hunter-chasers are not properly hunted and are former good steeplechasers who get older and find it easier to go hunter-chasing than continue sliding down the handicap in ordinary chases. I was shocked to find that the conditions of the Foxhunter's Chase at the Cheltenham Festival had no discrimination against former top race horses and several animals past their peak were allowed to win.

As I say Compton Lad was the genuine article. He had been extensively hunted while with my aunt Jackie Brutton who left me all her horses (all hunter-chasers). My aunt had been one of the first ladies to come to the fore in point-to-points and still at Harrow I once went to a point-to-point in the south with a school friend I was staying with in the holidays. To my amazement Aunt Jackie came up to me having won the ladies race. I had no idea how good she was. She was joint master of the North Cotswold Hunt for twenty years and had made her home at Compton Abdale, where she trained a number of very good hunter-chasers (one of which won the Foxhunters).

Unfortunately my aunt had a series of bad falls riding and the last one a simple fall in her stable yard left her unable to speak and badly impaired, although her brain was still functioning. The summer before her death was a dry and hot one and knowing she had not long to live her excellent stud groom (who went on to Princess Michael of Kent) allowed a number of young horses to run in point-to-points on bone hard going and many were broken down when I went to survey my new horses. Compton Lad was virtually the only one who was worth putting into training. So Compton Lad started with Fred Rimell, won a point-to-point and actually started favourite for the National Hunt chase where he fell early on. Michael Dickenson who took over was surrounded by family when I arrived on the scene. His father Tony had been a successful northern trainer and his mother Monica took a large part in the training. Much more formidable than Tony, you had to watch what you said. She was very quick to pick up stupid comments.

The Dickensons had an abundance of riding talent and that included a top-class amateur, Dermot Brown, who was the natural to partner Compton Lad. Dermot was the son of a notable Irish trainer, Liam Brown, and he soon proved his worth. One of the early successes was at Haydock Park, which turned out to be one of the most memorable days of my life as I learned Michael's other runner was owned by Angela Bell who was to become my second (and last) wife. I went with an old friend David Stern who, like me, didn't particularly like point-to-points, and preferred to go to a 'proper' race meeting. David and I headed for the upstairs members bar at Haydock where I had so many happy sessions with Robert Sangster. I had arranged to meet Michael there and he arrived with Angela who was greeted by David who knew her much better than I did. Compton Lad won easily and Angela's horse ran well without winning. We all had a very convivial day which resulted, a few months later, in my entering a second and very happy marriage with Angela.

Compton Lad won many of his races, although the Foxhunters at the Cheltenham Festival was to elude him. He should have won the race the following year, when in the lead and cruising, he made an uncharacteristic error three from home and unseated Dermot. Michael had insisted we watched the racing on television in the Weighing Room and was very nervous. The following race was the one when he had the first five in the Gold Cup, a feat which surely will never be repeated.

I did have another horse with Michael called Next Week, which ran in Angela's name and was a wedding present to her. He won first time out before having a bad injury and he did not race again.

Shortly afterwards Michael went to Manton as Robert Sangster's private trainer. Although Robert tried to give him every assistance, Michael missed his family and friends and the venture ended with Barry Hills taking his place and Michael eventually moving to America, where he trained successfully and was responsible for introducing a new all-weather surface, Tapeta, which he sold worldwide.

Philip Hobbs, who had trained Elaine Tully for Patricia Wilkins, trained the first foal from her for Patricia and I. Unfortunately he never reached a racecourse, having to be put down the day before he was due to run. Philip's wife, Sarah, was a great help when we were both guests of Richard and Lizzie Kelvin-Hughes, shooting grouse at Knarlsdale in Cumbria. I had just finished two months of intensive radiotherapy at the Royal Marsden on my prostrate and should never have accepted the invitation. Sarah and I were in an Amphicat to take us over the moor, which turned out to be extremely uncomfortable on very uneven ground. Just hang on to me said Sarah, which I did with great enthusiasm!

Paul Webber had, unknown to me, come into my life years before I sent him a horse. He had been one of a number of teenagers who had joined my son, Euan, on the sands of a famous south Wales resort. Euan had borrowed my new Range Rover and was under strict instructions from me not to let anyone else drive it. Nevertheless, he let a friend do so, who turned it over at high speed on the sands. Nobody was hurt but the car was badly damaged and instead of making sure the AA dealt with it, Euan rushed home to give me the bad news and face the music. He returned to find the Range Rover vandalised and everything of value taken.

I met Paul when he was assistant to Jeremy Hindley; Paul was so popular with the owners that Jeremy told me he had no need to go racing!

Years later Paul became my trainer of the second foal of Elaine Tully, a big filly who started life on the flat and came nearest to winning under a fine ride from Emma Ramsden (now Spencer) in a two-mile ladies race at Chester. She did win two races over hurdles but was disqualified in the second because Paul's head lad had given her the wrong bucket of food and at the enquiry he made the memorable statement that whatever they did to him would have less hurt than his owner's speech on the subject.

I forgave him and the filly, One Gulp, was to become the next he trained for me and an outstanding filly as well.

I should say at this point that one of the great things of being an owner of Paul's was that he tried to make racing fun, which is so important. He would go to a course like Uttoxeter, where at that time it was impossible to get a decent bottle of wine, and bring a superb picnic and a couple of bottles of excellent white wine. It came as a considerable shock when his marriage collapsed very unexpectedly to all but himself and he exchanged his lovely wife Fiona for another lovely lady, Coo, who, like Paul, had been in the group on the Pendine sands. Whilst his second marriage has been very happy, the divorce was inevitably costly to him.

All continued to go reasonably well on the horse front and One Gulp was potentially the best chaser I ever had. Like all her family, she had taken time to develop and her record of eleven runs for five wins, two involving black type, did little justice to the ability she was developing. Her breaking down alongside Big Bucks in the Long Walk Hurdle at Cheltenham, about three-quarters of a mile from the finish, was one of the worst racing days of my life though I was not there to see it, having decided that our Christmas shoot at Llanarmon had to have preference. I did watch the race on television and managed to get through to Paul, who did a noble job in saving the filly for breeding, as the injury was very severe. To make matters worse, Dominic Elsworth, her jockey, said he had never seen the filly going better when the breakdown occurred.

George Baker was assistant to Paul Webber and when he left to train himself, he took some staff with him. He became my last flat trainer, with two horses from my last flat mares. We had some exciting moments and quite a bit of place numbers, although winners rather eluded us. George also believed in racing being fun and his attractive and knowledgeable wife, Candida, was a great help to him. George is a keen shot and his first appearance at Llanarmon was memorable. We had heavy snow, which restricted our shooting to a few coverts, and the first was the highest of all, Stynog Wood. Four pheasants flew over George's head without a shot being fired and I had to shout, 'You are supposed to shoot at them.'

George had a spell at Whitsbury but found it very expensive and moved to Manton, as second independent trainer there and he has had some success, particularly in valuable handicaps.

I bracket **Jack** and **Linda Ramsden** together because although Linda held the licence, Jack did all the entries and evaluated the work the horses did. They were, in every sense of the word, a couple, when it came to training racehorses. Jack is also the only trainer I have ever had who was brutally honest about a horse's chance. A pessimist by nature, he would never fancy a horse unless he was convinced it had an excellent chance. He was also a highly successful punter, particularly when it came to laying horses, which he found to be more profitable than backing them – and the arrival of Betfair obviously helped him considerably. We all became great friends and when Jack bought a lovely house in the South of France, near Grasse, we went to stay with them. Unfortunately, Jack has a slightly restless nature and liked after a period to move on. The South of France house got sold and a mutual friend, who had holidayed with us there, rang me up to say, 'How dare Jack sell our lovely house in France.' The same restless nature caused him to give up training and move to France at a time when Linda was having some success. France did not work out and although they tried again to train, the owners had moved on and it did not really work out. I had a few horses with them which sadly were not much good but I did sell their owners one or two, the best being Far Removed, a half brother to Inglis Drever. His owner, Lord Petersham, was married for the second time to Anita Suffolk, previously married to the Earl of that name. Stunningly beautiful, she and Micky had stayed at Carden when I lived there.

When Jack and Linda gave up training we remained great friends and would go on holidays together and I usually stay with them whenever I went to Newmarket. Linda had the bad luck to be kicked by a pony, which led to whole series of operations which have badly affected her life. I very much hope that this lovely lady will find an answer to it.

Kim Bailey has been an acquaintance for many years; now he trains the second foal of One Gulp, Lady of Llanarmon, and has become a friend. Kim had had two excellent spells of training at top National Hunt level, with a spell in the wilderness in between. Now happily married for the second time and with wonderful facilities in Mark Vestey's estate, he is right at the top of the tree again. Lady of Llanarmon has not run yet and, like all the family, she is taking time to grow and mature. By Yeats, a record Ascot Gold Cup winner, she was never going to be an early sort but we are full of hope. She is superbly bred! My co-owner is Virginia Johnson, who is someone I have known since I was twenty, when I first took her out. Her formidable mother had other ideas for a husband for her, which ended our romance and she is now happily married for the second time to David Johnson, one of the best shots in the country.

I cannot finish this chapter without writing about **John Gosden**. Although I have never had a horse with him, we have been friends for many years. He inherited, as his travelling head lad, somebody I had found a job n racing, who was originally with Doug Francis and Jeremy Hindley took him on before he went to John Gosden. He left John and came back to train in Shropshire, but like many he struggled and seems to have left the trainers ranks. John has, of course, been immensely successful and this year I asked him for a horse to put in my 'Twelve to Follow' and he gave me Golden Horn and added Martlet.

I have been a member of the Twelve Club for more years than I care to remember. The members all choose twelve horses at the beginning of the flat season and back them against other members. There is a dinner in early March, when the prizes are distributed to the winners. Although I have never been the outright winner, I have received the prize for the most winning horses. But for John's two selections I would be bottom of the list this year and although I am not out of the wood yet, he may save me from receiving the trophy for 'bum of the year'. The club also has a very nice tie which very few members seem to wear, although Ian Balding and I often wear it to go racing.

John comes shooting every year to our family shoot at Llanarmon. Like David Johnson, he is an extremely fine shot and if he did it more regularly would compare with some of the great shots I have been privileged to shoot with. He is also extremely fit as I witnessed this year when he let his son shoot in the front row and took an outside gun, vaulting fences and bounding up the hill like the two-year-olds he trains.

The owner/trainer relationship can often be a difficult one – for obvious reasons – but I like to think that for the most part mine has been peaceful.

Chapter 13

Royal Ascot

Although the Royal Procession was started by George IV, Queen Victoria, carried it on with great enthusiasm. George IV had left her an excellent legacy. He had inaugurated an annual dinner at which the Royal meeting was fully discussed and, as most of the good and great in racing were invited to the dinner, much was said which led to improvements in the course and increases in the prizes given. After the King's death, the Queen headed the seven carriages which drove up the new mile. Her Majesty was attired in a pink silk slip over which was a lace dress and she wore a white gauze pole bonnet trimmed with pink ribbons. The Queen seemed to be very interested in the races and in fact her enthusiasm did much to save the royal meeting as the number of entries was declining and the crowd was smaller than usual. It was at this point that a major grandstand was constructed and a company was formed to finance it. The course saw major improvements with the turf being re-laid on new sub-soil.

The Royal Procession of 1847 had nine coaches, the first conveyed the Queen, the Grand Duchess of Saxe-Weimar, the Grand Duke Constantine of Russia and the Prince of Lucca. The second; Prince Albert, the Grand Duke of Saxe-Weimar, Prince George and Prince Edward of Saxe-Weimar. The third; the Duchess of Sutherland, Vicountess Carring, Baron de Brusnow (the Russian minister) and the Duke of Norfolk. The other six coaches conveyed a whole string of notables. The Queen's Vase was exhibited in front of the Stewards Stand; the Emperor's Cup and the Hunt Cup in the Salon of the Grand Stand. Her Majesty was reportedly in high spirits and participated in the awards for the day, including the sweepstakes. The richest race, the Ascot Stakes was won by Woodpigeon by a neck at 15/1.

The Prince of Wales took an enormous interest in horse racing and did much to further the sport. Although his mother had supported Ascot, she did not approve of Bertie owning horses and he was careful to start in a small way. The Jockey Club had made him a member early and handled him cleverly, letting him participate in debates and encouraging him in every way. His mother's refusal to let him see State papers left him with a lot of free time and his horse owning friends gave him the encouragement lacking in his immediate family.

Prince Albert's death in 1861 led to the Monarch withdrawing from the Royal meeting: indeed she never attended another race meeting. Though she continued her patronage of the meeting, it was left to her eldest son to lead the Royal Procession and the stream of European royalty who continued to attend the meeting. The Prince of Wales Stakes was a new race, worth £1,500, a large increase in prize money and improvements continued to the stands and a new stand, the Alexandra Stand, was built. In 1967, though the trustees found themselves short of money and had to borrow, giving personal guarantees. A writer at the time wrote: 'It must not be thought that the alterations pleased everybody and the additional fees pleased none.' The latter referred to the fees the trustees tried to charge for entrance to the paddock.

The arrival of the railway helped to swell the crowds during the later part of the nineteenth century. It is worth recalling the words of a scribe of the time writing about the Diamond Jubilee of 1897 a few years later:

> In the Royal Procession were the Prince and Princess of Wales, the Duke of Saxe-Coburg and Gothia, the Princess Victoria of Wales, the Duke and Duchess of York, Prince Albert of Schleswig-Holstein, the Crown Prince of Denmark, the Duke of Cambridge and Prince Christian. They came in five carriages, each drawn by four horses with postilions. A long roll of cheering announces that the Prince and Princess of Wales have arrived and the cheering only ceases when the party are safely ensconced in the Royal Stand. As the cheering dies down the bell rings for the first race and the day's business commences.

In the popular estimate the pre-race luncheon is the most popular part of the day. The dresses at Ascot are a characteristic feature and it would not be Ascot were not the lawns and enclosures filled with graceful women in beautiful costumes – but luncheon is even more enjoyed. Hospitality is remarkable during the five days racing and pervades all classes of society represented. The Turf and other clubs welcome a large circle to their elegant repasts and the roofs of the coaches from one end of the club enclosure to the other afford one huge banquet. The private luncheon rooms in the Grandstand are the scene of many pleasant parties and the large dining halls on the lawn at the back of the Grandstand are well patronised and during the lunch hour proper are full to overflowing. Another of the great features of Royal Ascot are the picnics which take place all over the course. The places in Car

Park No.1 are still jealously guarded and picnics abound there and in the Owners and Trainers Car Park, which is the scene of tremendous activity before and after racing. I have always tried to get a place there, close to Barry and Charles Hills and Nick Henderson, who park close together. My driver was very friendly with Mark Johnston's driver, who having not long ago retired, sadly died recently. You certainly need a driver at Ascot. After racing the Owners and Trainers Car Park is one long cocktail party at which I am pleased to say a lot of wine from the company I co-founded and am chairman of gets consumed. When the New Stand was built Raymond Mould said, 'At least they have left us the Car Park, why don't we get a large screen and never move out of it!'

The two Club tents I used to lunch in, Whites and the Turf Club, are as popular as ever. In fact the meeting is thriving again after a hiccup when some regulars stopped going, after the new stand was built.

In the period between the wars and also after World War Two, there was one strict rule that divorcees could not use the Royal Enclosure. When I started going to the Royal Enclosure there were always one or two wearing badges that did not have their own names. They always looked a bit shifty.

The five days that make up the Royal Meeting are unquestionably the best five days of racing anywhere in the world. The cards cover all distances in racing and cater for all age groups of horses. The very best day is possibly the first, when the meeting starts off with the Queen Anne Stakes, a mile race for older horses, over the straight course. It is usually won by a very good older horse. The next race, the Coventry, is a Group 2, for two-year-olds, over six furlongs and the two following: The King's Stand, for older sprinters, and the St James's Palace, over a mile on the round course for three-year-olds only, both of which are Group Ones. Then follows the Ascot Stakes for older handicappers, over two-and-a-half miles the same distance as the Gold Cup – and the Windsor Castle Cup – a Listed race for two-year-olds, over five furlongs.

The meeting very sensibly only has six races in the day, unlike most other courses who usually have seven, but all five days are full of top-class Pattern races and I cannot fault the five cards, which are varied and full of interest from first to last. The last race is actually the Queen Alexandra, the longest race in the calendar, hated by some purists and loved by people like me who like to try and pick out a winner.

Ascot has changed hugely since I first started going some sixty years ago. Because I was having to work a strict five-day week, I could only go on 'Heath' day in my early years. Heath day was not part of the Royal meeting, there was no procession and it was a jolly relaxed day with no Royal Enclosure and you just paid a normal entry fee to attend. When my children went to their first schools, both just happened to be at Ascot. My eldest, Euan, went to Heatherdown, run by James Edwards and his wife, and his two years younger sister, Sara, went to St Mary's, Ascot, a Catholic girl's school, run by nuns with a rather fierce one, Mother Bridget, as the Headmistress. Whilst I had no trouble getting Euan into Heatherdown, my efforts with St Mary's were very different. I turned up with my wife the week before Royal Ascot and was firmly told by the elderly nun deputising for Mother Bridget that there was little chance of a place but she would show us around if we wished.

We agreed and both of us were impressed by the facilities and the good manners of the pupils and went away saddened by the fact we were not going to get a place, though we had been introduced to Mother Bridget just before we left. I had said that I was coming for the Royal week's racing and that I had a horse, Precipice Wood, who would run well in the Gold Cup. A few days after winning the race I received a letter from Mother Bridget to say that she would be able to give Sara a place after all. Sadly, Sara never liked the school, coming back after the first term to say that if the nuns at St Mary's represented religion, she wanted nothing to do with it, as they were the most two-faced lot she had ever come across. She left school aged sixteen, but I am told it is no longer run by nuns and is now quite different. Euan did well at Heatherdown and his brother, Christopher, went there as well and in fact is a near contemporary of David Cameron. We all used to go to Sports Day, where after a picnic lunch the children would compete and a parents race would finish the festivities. The Royals, who were now sending their boys to Heatherdown, did not go to the races on Heath day and had their picnic amongst us and I always felt there was a distinct lack of alcohol compared to our picnic which had plenty of wine. On one occasion, Euan arrived from Harrow to join us and insisted I took him to the race meeting instead of the sports. We duly set off but an imperious looking Mrs Edwards was waiting for a late Royal and furiously waved us to go the back way. Christopher always said his last term was ruined because of the two of us being caught going racing.

I have to be honest and say that I much preferred the course before the new stand and paddock were built. The old stand was built by Wimpey and David Marchwood's father had been taken on by Wimpey as a sales director. He had a video made during the construction which he would show to other racecourses who were envisaging new stands. The old stand had a homely feel about it, which it totally lacking in the current monstrosity. Worse still was the loss of the wonderful old paddock and saddling enclosure. I can only echo the words of Barry

Hills in a recent magazine article, who was saddened by the disbanding of the old paddock. He wrote to the then Queen's representative at Ascot, The Duke of Devonshire, and asked him how he would feel if the Cascade at Chatsworth was done away with and unsurprisingly didn't receive a reply. He finished the paragraph with the words: 'What the young people didn't see before they won't miss.' In fact the meeting is more popular than ever with nearly 300,000 people attending this year.

The Royal Procession is also more popular than ever, and I am told off the record that there is competition amongst the senior Royals to get into the front carriages. The Duke of Edinburgh at ninety-four looks quite cheerful these days and his Aston Martin is no longer conspicuously outside to whisk him away. It is, of course, Her Majesty who makes the meeting and her energy, good humour and obvious enjoyment of seeing wonderful horses is positively infectious.

One of the advantages of the new stand for the Royals is that they are not now overlooked by the Jockey Club, who had the privilege in the former stand of being able to overlook the Royal Box and see most of what went on inside it.

The Royal Enclosure is, frankly, not what it used to be and what I feel is a pity, the Paddock lacks the charm of the old one, although those gathered around it can now see the Royal Procession as it completes its journey from Windsor Castle and lets Her Majesty's dismount. The separation of the Royal Enclosure from the rest of the course is much less pronounced and in the old days the one place to meet those not blessed with a Royal Enclosure Badge was the Irish Bar, strategically placed between the old paddock and the saddling enclosure. The bar had quite a large restaurant attached to it and was my home for many years until it was transformed into the dining room for the Ascot Racing Club. Robert Sangster's old box is still standing but no longer overlooks the Paddock but it is near the Jockey Club's second box for drinks during the day.

The Royal meeting has been a lucky one for me; I have won four of their races and should have won a fifth, The Ascot Stakes, won by our pacemaker instead. To win the Gold Cup, aged thirty-nine, was one of my lifetime's great thrills.

Chapter 14

Betting

I have gained enormous pleasure from backing horses, though I suspect over the years the bookmaking fraternity are fairly well in front. I have some memorable moments, my first being my jackpot win (I was one of three), on Lincoln day in the early sixties. £10,928.15 may not sound an enormous amount of money but in those days it certainly was and indeed my first house in Cheshire, which recently sold for nearly two million pounds, actually cost me less.

The second great moment was my bet of forty thousand to two placed with Michael Simmonds of Heathorns in 1983, before Cormorant Wood won the Benson and Hedges (now Juddmonte) International Stakes at York's Ebor meeting. The bet was made as insurance against her winning the race as her value would increase considerably – and I had already sold a half share – if she was to win. In fact she broke down after winning the race so the bet was a small consolation. I don't suppose Michael Simmonds saw it that way.

There are different types of punters betting on horse racing. Those who go racing occasionally and spice up the day by having a few small bets, those who go to betting shops regularly to cheer up their day and those who go racing regularly and study form assiduously. Obviously there are a lot of punters who don't fit any of those categories.

There are many rules one should follow when backing horses and two of them are golden. One you must control your gambling, not let it control you. This applies to all addictions and betting is no different in this respect from alcoholism, smoking or drugs. Secondly, do not bet on every race. That is the quickest way to the poor house. The slogan, it's more fun if you have money on it, may be true but nobody can back winners all the time.

I have known two betting addicts well. The first, Charles Benson, succeeded Clive Graham as the Scout of the *Daily Express*. He joined a paper whose other racing correspondent, Peter O'Sullivan, was to become famous as a commentator. Both men love betting but whereas Benson was hopelessly addicted, O'Sullivan controlled his and never had an overdraft. When I wrote my obituary of Charles for the *Daily*

Telegraph, I wanted to put in the story his girlfriend for seven years told me, which was that Charles was the nicest person in the World until he ran out of betting money when he would grovel to people he normally wouldn't bother with if he thought they would lend him money. Sadly this was the one story in my copy the *Telegraph* did not include.

The second major addict, John Slesinger, was not dissimilar. Born into a very rich family (his father was Sir Gordon Richards's London doctor), he went through a business his godfather had left him before founding a travel agency I was stupid enough to get my old family company to purchase. We were starting an overseas company at the time and could give it a lot of business. I could not understand why it didn't make a modest profit and put it up for sale. The then chief executive of Wickes was a prospective buyer and asked if he could have access to the travel agency books. He came back two days later and said John Slesinger is a hopeless backer of horses. He has to have betting money and he is also in charge of the till! He bought the agency and I have never discovered what happened to it or John subsequently.

Many readers will not have 'form books' but to any serious followers I thoroughly recommend the Flat and Jumps books which have weekly instalments which are put into the loose leaf covers. I confess to spending hours buried in the form books and often spend extra time in the morning reading them. The comments by experts writing up past form are very useful and have saved me from disaster on numerous occasions.

In my old age I have found backing horses over the jumps easier than the flat. Firstly, there is no draw which can make an enormous difference to a horse's chances on the flat. Also there is not usually the same difference in winter ground that one gets on the flat, where watering is essential for many courses in mid-summer. The going description 'good to firm' can mean different things to Clerks of the Courses. My old friend, Stanley Clarke, whose property company bought Uttoxeter Racecourse, used to instruct his Clerk of the Course that he had to have 'good' in the going report however firm the ground was. Paul Webber and I had a runner at an evening meeting and when we got there the first person I ran into was A.P. McCoy. 'What's the going like, champ?' I said. 'It's mostly hard with a few firm patches' was the answer. Our horse was one of several withdrawals and no guesses as to the winning jockey of the race. I still have no regrets withdrawing the horse, although we were forecast to be five to two on. I once saw a very good horse of mine break down after winning easily, a ten thousand pound novice race at Hexham. Good horses should not run on very firm ground.

Jumps racing now goes on all year round but I tend to avoid betting on jumps racing in the summer and stick to the flat. The one time I try not to back flat horses is at the beginning of the flat season, when form is very topsey turvey and I hate the all-weather.

The two great jumps races for me are the Gold Cup and the Grand National. This year's results were a salutary lesson, as I should have backed both winners but failed to do so. Mark Bradstock and wife, Sara, are two lovely people, who are literally dedicated to their horses. Mark's father, David, and I shot grouse at Swinton together for many years and both of us were great friends of David Swinton and Tim Kitson, who ran our team. David Swinton loved having his friends shooting and the charges were well below a normal top Yorkshire moor. David Bradstock was a highly successful businessman but not a great shot, whereas son, Mark, was very good indeed. I should have known that their decision to go for the Gold Cup with Coneygree, a novice which had only run four times over fences, was not made lightly. Although most of the media were sceptical, to put it mildly, that a novice could win jump racing's premier distance race, he was quite strongly supported in the betting market, another strong pointer which I should not have ignored. I have for many years gone to the Gold Cup with my good friend Raymond Mould, whose love affair with Cheltenham goes back to his late wife, Jenny, who was a passionate supporter of her racehorses. We had our usual excellent cold lunch and watched the race on television. Nobody cheered louder for Coneygree than I did, although I had backed Silviniaco Conti for the third year running. I had convinced myself that the going between the last when Silviniaco Conti came over first and failed to reach a place last year was due to the ground being much faster for those who came wide on the far side. However, I did not make the mistake of deserting Silviniaco Conti at Aintree, where he was never really in danger of being defeated and my winnings there more than made up for the Cheltenham losses. Never was the phrase, 'horses for courses' more true! I left after the fifth race and who should I run into between the entrance to the members and the car, Sara Bradstock and two stable staff. They looked totally elated and had obviously been overseeing Coneygree's departure. Such was the Moulds hospitality that I temporarily forgot Sara's christian name and she plainly didn't place me either, as I shouted my 'well done' at her.

I should of course have backed Many Clouds at Aintree but I had not done sufficient homework on the race and my main bet was Shutthefrontdoor, ridden by A.P. McCoy and supposedly due to start at a ridiculously poor price. In fact, again the market should have told me that the excellent price I got meant that there were concerns. I was further encouraged that Jonjo O'Neill, having greeted me enthusiastically at Haydock seven days before, had given him as his nap for Aintree. If he didn't know the horse didn't stay, why should I?

My betting mentor, Jack Ramsden, rang me the Monday after to announce that, not only had he backed Many Clouds and the American winner of the Masters Golf, but that he stupidly had not doubled them. I was so angry I nearly put the phone down on him, but he was right, Many Clouds should have been backed at twenty-five to one. He was a class horse with a very reasonable weight and he stayed, which A.P. McCoy's horse didn't. Many Clouds had won the Hennessy and although a long price at twenty-five to one, actually forty to one earlier in the day, he was eminently backable. The race has changed totally as a result of the RSPCA and the media, the fences are much softer and easier and the only problem is they are jumped at much greater speed. This does lead to some very tired horses at the end of the race and despite the hosing down and veterinary treatment, it is not good news when the winner does not go straight into the winner's enclosure. Oliver Sherwood, who also loves his horses (who doesn't?) could hardly answer the questions put to him after the race, so great was his concern for the winner's wellbeing but all was well in the end, the horse finally being paraded and the champagne could be hosed down (like the horse!).

The National has been a great race for me over the years. I have, in the distant past, twice backed the winner at a hundred to one, Nicholas Silver before he won at Cheltenham, landed the race when the ground was far faster than it would ever be today. Aintree's marvellous water system can now ensure the going is no worse than genuinely good. I also backed Ayala, who won in 1963, at a hundred to one, trained by Lester Piggott's father for celebrity hairdresser, Peter Raymond, also known as Teasy Weasy. Another big win was on Raymond Mould's horse, Bindaree. Raymond had stayed with me for some years for Aintree and like me is not a fan of the 'roof' in the Princess Royal Stand, where for some years I had a large box. Although the box could contain nearly forty people, only three were left in it to watch the race, Raymond, who does not bet, Caroline and the local golf professional, Ellis Jones, who does. Ellis had backed the second, What's Up Boys, and got more and more excited, shouting his horse home. He was quite shocked when Raymond languidly said a hundred or maybe two hundred yards from the winning post, 'I think mine is going to win.' Ellis got mercilessly teased as he still hadn't realised that Raymond actually owned the winner. In fact Bindaree changed the course of top trainer, Nigel Twiston-Davies's life, as he was about to retire from training and Bindaree did us all a great favour.

The arrival of Betfair has had a dramatic effect on the betting market. Jack Ramsden has for years been saying that the easiest way to make money is to lay favourites which are far too short a price and of course he can now do that openly on Betfair. Although I had an account with them, I am far too old to work the modern technology and soon went back to my traditional bookmakers. Nor am I a fan of laying horses, I have only laid two or three in my life and the last one was a total disaster. Nicky Henderson had come to stay for a Bangor-on-Dee meeting and I had opened some very good Bordeaux in his honour, which both of us had taken on board in some quantity. The following day we headed for Bangor, where I was chairman at the time, and Nicky said, 'I will definitely win the first but I will be odds on.' Not for the first time, I had a large bet at odds on, only to see the horse get well beaten (it might have fallen). Nicky then said, 'Please don't get out on my other runner owned by the Queen Mother, as I really don't think it will win.' I then said, 'Can I lay it Nicky?' and he said, a trifle reluctantly, 'If you must.' The bookies couldn't wait to take my laying the horse as everybody else seemed to be backing it. When it sailed into the lead two fences from home, I said, 'Are you sure about this Nicky?' I didn't get a reply. Of course it won by the proverbial street and I had to pretend I was as delighted by the Royal win as the rest of the course, who had thrown their hats in the air with great enthusiasm. There was a sequel to this story as I received an extremely nice tie from Nicky in the post a few days later. We were both playing in the wonderful golf tournament Doncaster Bloodstock ran in Scotland and on the first evening I put the tie on, Mick Fitzgerald, also playing in the tournament, looked at the tie rather sadly and said to Nicky, 'You really shouldn't have given Mr Bobby that tie – it's far too close to the Queen Mother's colours for him to enjoy it!'

Backers on the flat really must study the draw. In races up to a mile, with big fields, it can make an enormous difference and watering can often increase the bias. Backing ante-post can be very dangerous until a race reveals whether there is major bias.

At Chester, my home racecourse, a low draw favours horses in races up to seven furlongs, although fresh ground in the straight can make it possible for a jockey with a high draw to come late up the far rails. The important thing is not to go wide on the bend into the final short straight and lose a lot of ground. Last year, in a two-year-old race with nine runners, numbers eight and nine were first and second.

Many good judges find paddock appearance very important and a horse who looks really well in him or herself should certainly be taken into account – but remember, like humans, some horses sweat more easily than others.

After years of trying to beat the bookmakers, I offer the following advice: try and not bet odds on, beware of too many each-way bets, as bookies' odds on places are generally poor, don't increase your bets to try and recover losses, be careful of the draw on the flat, take the going into consideration and above all feel you are in control and have fun.

Chapter 15

The Media

The media has always been extremely important to ensure the popularity of racing and hopefully racing will continue to be equally as important to the media. The shape of both the press and television coverage has changed over the sixty plus years of my racing life. Although the main daily papers remain much the same the circulation of the *Daily Express* is way down on the Beaverbrook years when Clive Graham and Peter O'Sullivan were the most influential racing duo on any newspaper. The television scenario is completely altered. The BBC have left the sport, preferring football, which has become extremely expensive to sponsor. Sixty years ago nobody could envisage this happening and a succession of supremos in the BBC were courted by the Jockey Club and the main racecourses. When I joined the board of Aintree the two most important sets of people were our sponsors, Seagrams, and the BBC.

In the early days of televised racing I knew several of the leading players. Peter Dimmock and I had several dinners together. He had joined the BBC just after the war and soon became manager for outside broadcasts on the BBC television. In his book *Calling the Horses* Peter O'Sullivan writes of working under Dimmock and the lack of proper commentating boxes and the malfunctions of much of the equipment. Peter was to succeed Raymond Glendenning as the outside broadcaster of major racing events. The entry of ITV in competition to the BBC was to benefit the racing industry enormously. The infighting between them ensured that good prices were to be paid for all the main race meetings, the only exception being Chester, to whom Channel Four refused to pay a reasonable fee. This did have one advantage, that we could argue with them over the starting time for racing. Channel Four had a popular programme, Countdown, which started at three twenty and all racing had to finish before then. This meant that they wanted to start much earlier than racecourses would have liked and Chester was the only course that took them on as all the other large courses felt that television was so vital to attract sponsors that they gave in totally to Channel Four's demands. Chester got some sneers from the media who forgot that at the May meeting the boxes, marquees etc. were major sources of revenue and that most of the racegoers in them actually wanted a decent lunch before racing. Many of Chester's sponsors were loyal and would have remained anyway had Channel Four carried out their threat not to cover the meeting at all. Although it never came to that, there were many anxious moments.

When I joined the board at Aintree it became obvious that the two most important tasks for the racecourse were to keep the sponsor happy and to extract the maximum from the BBC – the fees to televise the National were enormous. All Aintree's profits were earned at the one three-day meeting, with the Grand National on Saturday, the final day. Although we tried Autumn meetings and an evening meeting in early May, they were not a financial success.

A great deal of effort went into increasing the television payments. Although commercial television had taken over many leading races the BBC were determined to hang on to the National Meeting, though there was the worry that the new BBC directors would change their minds and Peter Daresbury was constantly trying to woo them. Many events were laid on to bring us closer together and two I remember well were a weekend at Herez in Spain where, after a heavy dinner, Flamenco dancers gave an excellent cabaret, the only problem being that we were all invited onto the dance floor to join them. Des Lynham was the first to leap on to the floor but Clare Balding and I both hid behind two pillars until we were spotted by Des, who insisted that we joined the fun. My partner saved the day by whispering 'just follow me' and all was well. The other occasion was a dinner in Ireland at The Curragh. The following morning I got up at the crack of dawn to show Sue Barker an early morning gallop of a leading trainer. After the return flight I told Peter Daresbury that I thought he should have insisted on two pilots instead of the one who flew us. He thought I was being ridiculous. The very next flight landing afterwards with one pilot plunged into the Mersey killing all on board!

Although fatalities at Aintree were not greatly different to any other course, they seemed to draw out the antis and the vast television audience which attracts many who do not normally watch racing, to react with horror whenever a horse had to be put down. Racing correspondents who understand that accidents can happen in every form of sport involving horses would have written sensibly on the subject had it not been for pressure from their editors, who sensed an increase in sales could result from making accidents at Aintree into sensations. The two fatalities in the 2011 and 2012 races really accelerated the pressure and the fact that it was particularly warm during the first and a Gold

Cup winner involved in the second made things much worse. We tried everything to make the famous fences safer. Peter and I went to look at the modified Becher's Brook, where a trickle of water stood in place of the brook where Captain Becher sheltered underneath the fence and after I had left the board the decision was made to alter the cores of the fences and make them much softer which has certainly resulted in less fallers as horses can brush through the top. This allied with Aintree's excellent watering system, which ensures the going is never worse than Good, has completely altered the race. The public probably prefer seeing many less fallers but there is a downside in that the warm conditions which now often occur and the speed with which the fences are now jumped can lead to the horses finishing overheated and distressed. This happened this year when the winner failed to immediately come into the winner's enclosure; his trainer, Oliver Sherwood, was far too worried to show the normal elation he would have felt.

Only one daily racing paper remains, the *Racing Post*, owned by the rulers of Dubai, who have done so much for British flat racing and who also sponsor Channel Four Racing. The *Racing Post* is expensive at £2.20 but it is an absolute necessity for dedicated horse racing fans. It covers all parts of horse racing and includes greyhound racing and the betting on most other sports. It is the only paper which prints the four day entries and the flat declarations the day before racing. Its tipping meets with mixed fortunes, though columns like 'Pricewise' have a good reputation.

All the other daily papers print all the racecards for the day though the journalist's contributions have declined over the years, particularly in the tabloids. The much admired Alan Lee writes a daily column in *The Times*, whilst Tom Peacock and Marcus Armitage cover racing for the *Daily Telegraph*, with an occasional but always interesting column from Charlie Brooks. Claude Duval who I used to meet for a glass of beer before racing at Newmarket still writes for the *Sun* and Marcus Townsend for the *Daily Mail*. Sadly the one London evening paper, the *Evening Standard*, now revived as a free newspaper, dependent on advertising, has no racing content.

Never have horseracing followers had better television coverage. The BBC has retired from the scene now dominated by Channel Four, whose extremely professional team go from strength to strength. Clare Balding, who used to head it, now only makes an occasional appearance, although she does appear for Royal Ascot. Nick Luck leads the team for most other days and is becoming increasingly popular. Regulars include Mick Fitzgerald, Jim McGrath and Emma Spencer. John McCririck has completely vanished from the screen and his place has been taken by Tanya Stevenson.

The other two racing channels are: Racing UK, which covers most of the larger courses and At the Races, irreverently known by some of us as 'All the Rubbish'. Racing UK needed a subscription from viewers although it does have other benefits, but At the Races is free to air.

Sadly Peter O'Sullivan is no longer with us. His commentaries on the Grand National over fifty years are legendary and nobody has remotely matched his expertise in this department. Peter was a true colossus. In his youth he was a fearless punter and he must have been successful because he claimed never to have an overdraft. He wrote an excellent column in the *Daily Express*, first with Clive Graham and then with Charles Benson. His book *Calling the Horses* has twenty-six references to Graham and two to Benson which perhaps shows his opinion on the merits of his two colleagues.

I don't listen to car radios much but I must refer to one Cheltenham when Inglis Drever had one of his three World Hurdle wins. Richard Pitman saw me and asked me to do an interview, thinking I might get a large audience for the row I was having with the Thoroughbred Breeders Association over their refusal to give Inglis Drever breeders prizes, I waxed loudly on the subject for a couple of minutes. Richard Pitman thanked me and I went back into the Turf Club tent where I talked about my interview. 'Oh he works for local radio,' said somebody, 'you may get a few hundred listen to you if you're lucky'!

In general, the media gives generous coverage to the sport. Long may this continue!